CW01512324

UNDERSTANDING EGO DEFENSE MECHANISMS

A Guide for Educators

JOHN BUCKLEY PHD

Understanding Ego Defense Mechanisms

A Guide for Educators

Copyright: HSM Publishing, London, 2019

ACKNOWLEDGMENTS

The more psychology I read and the greater understanding I get, the more I realize how lucky I was with the parents I had. The emotional stability they provided and the opportunities they gave me, mean that when life throws the curve-balls I am in a much better place to deal with them. Growing up, I may not have realized this, but I know it now. So, a big thank you to my awesome parents, Ken and Nella.

And a big thank-you to my fellow trainers who have helped me over the years to deal with issues in the classroom, when I was blind to what was happening. And in that vein, a big apology to the students who suffered: I am sorry I didn't understand what you were going through.

Sincere thanks to my dear friends Dawn Starling and Judy Saba, for checking the manuscript for obvious errors. I owe you both a glass of wine. I owe you a lot more, for all the support you have given me over the years.

And to you dear reader, thanks for wanting to learn and for placing trust in me to help you.

FORWARD

O nce in a while you come across a book that not only is imbued with information, but that delivers that information in an easily digestible and enthralling way. John Buckley has done what many before have attempted – to take on the indisputable Freudian concept of 'ego defense mechanisms' and reimagine them for those of us who really seek applied understanding in place of academic gymnastics. John's experience spans many disciplines and his exceptional teaching style (I know this from personal experience of his programs) has necessitated this in depth and meaningful exploration of what many in the past have placed in the too hard basket.

In the many contexts in which we find ourselves the one common element is that human beings are complex, diverse and continually evolving. The way that personal, interpersonal and communal evolution occurs on a platform of global, environmental, technological and spiritual tsunamis, influences every aspect of our being. The place and pace at which we understand, manage and even conquer our ego defense mechanisms has become essential and is no longer optional. The critical nature of capturing them in the process of learning, places their importance on a whole other level. If a police officer, let's say, is confronted by a scenario in a training context that challenges their sense of self, then often one of three things happens. The officer either rejects the impact, or engages the possibility, or walks away from the training.

The recipe for an effective trainer contains a vital ingredient that if left out will undoubtedly render the session equivalent to a failed souffle – flat and inedible!!!

That vital ingredient is the ability of the trainer/educator to work with what is presented in the context of the learning experience, that being both the content and what is triggered in the learner.

Working in the policing context has allowed me to reflect on this, as I read through John's manuscript. Every day, the safety, decision making, self-awareness and response choices are impacted by these little beings within us that attempt to save us from pain, delude us from truth or protect us from the self or other. To see defense mechanisms as normal is at one end of the continuum. To allow them, consciously or unconsciously, to control the above is at the other end. As John so rightly states in this book, "they help us keep painful emotions, thoughts and fears outside of our awareness" My experience as a cross cultural psychologist has taught me that defense mechanisms, in some extreme situations, have also helped certain individuals to survive.

I recall the story of Lee, a survivor of torture and trauma, who according to his own word, had never played golf in his life. He recounted to me the many years he was held in captivity and, under the regime of the time, he had been tortured repeatedly. The only access to the real world was a peep hole in his cell wall that allowed him to see the television screen in an adjoining room, where his torturers often gathered. For some unknown reason it would always be on a channel that relayed lengthy golf tournaments. Lee would watch the tournaments, recreate and practice the moves in his head, and would try to imagine playing golf. It came to pass that when he was being tortured, Lee would go "somewhere else in his head" It was an unconscious response to pain, and for Lee, served to block out the horrendous pain of his very real torture. He told me he recalled that he would play golf in his head over and over and by doing this he would not feel the physical pain and more importantly he would avoid further psychological pain.

Lee developed the defense mechanism we know as dissociation. He had and continued to, detach from reality. The enduring nature of this detachment meant that when he escaped from the torture context and was in a safe place of asylum, he struggled to create connection and had to re-learn different coping strategies. I vividly recall Lee and the glazed look that would take over him, when therapy touched on a painful memory or association of one.

The interesting twist to Lee's story, is that within months of seeking asylum in what is now his new country of residence, he won a local golf tournament, even though he had never physically played golf. The power of recreating and replaying golf moves in his head, resulted in him replicating them in the real world. The experience of defense mechanisms as inhibitors is equally as powerful when awareness of them and the ability to recognize them, enables recovery and learning.

In this book, the ability to traverse the numerous ego defense mechanisms and to read the skillful analogies and examples that John has included to illustrate them, makes it possible to explore their presence within the observations you may engage. What this book clearly articulates is essential. Firstly, that defense mechanisms are present and through exploring the plethora that exist and illustrating them through applied examples, we see how they can help in understanding why we do what we do. Secondly, in considering ego defense mechanisms in the context of education, training, learning and development, this book will provide you as educator, learner, practitioner or other, with critical insights as to how they come in to play in the adult learning setting and broader human interactions.

So, whether you have picked up this book as a text, a teaching aide, a bedtime companion, or because you want to get to the bottom of your own behavior, this is about the only book, that I'm aware of, that will take you to the depths of ego defense mechanisms without requiring a DSM (the bible of psychiatry) to make sense of it.

John Buckley has captured and shared with us a snippet of his limitless experience, as well as his training, learning and education prowess in this fantastic book. He has brought to the forefront what we often see as an added extra and he has skillfully built this book into a useful revealing and relevant resource. Sorry Freud, but this now is my 'go to' on ego defense mechanisms. Enjoy the read…

Judy Saba

2010 Churchill Fellow

Registered Cross Cultural Psychologist

Applied Diversity and Human Rights Trainer (NSW Police Force)

Adjunct Fellow, Western Sydney University, Australia

Self-Confessed Foodie and Gourmet Safari Guide

Author's Note

A book seems like a lot of effort to try and explain one, arguably minor, concept in psychology, let alone one which is disputed by some. However, the subject addressed here is a problem I encounter in delivering training on such a regular basis I thought it would be worth the effort. While this book was originally intended to be for police officers and the roles they undertake, I hope that others will find it useful in understanding the concepts, and in identifying when these concepts are at play in real life situations.

This book comes after many years of delivering training to police officers and others, who are being asked to undertake high stress/high risk roles. When attempting to deliver new knowledge, what is often apparent is that police officers can be very resistant to change, especially when it comes to creating a consistent and lasting change in their behavior. What is more concerning is that these officers are being trained for roles where life and death decisions can occur on a regular basis and where unbiased, logical decision making, is critical. One would think given the risks involved these officers would be highly motivated to learn and many are. However, some just hit a wall.

After years of observation it became obvious that one of the primary factors for this resistance to change stems from them defending their ego. Police officers are confident individuals; their role requires them to be so and shapes them to be so. As years pass many become certain of who they are and certain they are 'right' about any topic they are likely to encounter. In addition, much of this defending of the ego was done at an unconscious level with many officers, blind to the fact as to how they were behaving. In listening to how they dealt with critique it became more and more apparent that ego defense mechanisms were often and inappropriately at play. These defense mechanisms played a significant part in creating a barrier to learning about new concepts and ideas. Without learning, change in behavior is all but impossible. Hence, I thought I would try and write something to address the issue.

Once I got started it seemed a shame to limit it solely to a restricted audience. So here it is, and I hope it helps whatever your reason was for buying it.

John, March 2019, London

Before you build your walls so strong, just remember that the only difference between a castle and a prison, is that with a prison, someone can let you leave.

Contents

1 - BACKGROUND

"I believe what I believe to make life less terrifying. That's all beliefs are; stories we tell ourselves to stop being afraid. Beliefs have very little to do with the truth."

The End of the World Running Club - Adrian J Walker

1.1 Introduction

The primary focus of this book is 'defense mechanisms', sometimes referred to as 'ego defense mechanisms.' While many may be familiar with these terms and have a general understanding of their meaning, the intent here is to provide a more detailed understanding and one which can help negate some of the more destructive aspects of utilizing these mechanisms.

While knowledge can never guarantee change, it is hoped that a better understanding of the nature of defense mechanisms and how they impact on our behavior will, for some at least, make changing their behavior an easier path to follow. That said, it would be foolish not to acknowledge how deep the origins of defense mechanisms can be. For many people the circumstances of their upbringing and other life events can mean that the very defense mechanisms that are present to protect us, can become a very destructive force in our life.

While a better understanding of defenses is developmental for most people, for some it can be quite traumatic. As we will see later, the very nature of some of the defense mechanisms we employ means that we may have buried experiences deep within our psyche. Some of those experiences can be very painful and can be buried very deep. For example: memories of childhood abuse are not the sort of thing we want at the front of our mind every day and are very typical of the type of thing we hide with defense mechanisms. We want to avoid pain, so we put it away from us. Though this is essentially the function of a defense mechanism and may seem like a good thing, what it often means is that we are merely putting a sticking plaster over a festering wound. Our everyday behavior remains impacted by the childhood trauma.

Defense mechanisms filter out things we may not want to recognize, and they can change our perception so things we are encountering become more comfortable for us. Defense mechanisms can also distort reality and in doing so can cause us problems in our daily life. In some ways they keep us from making a clear judgement about events and what is real. The way in which they distort our perception of reality often draws us into conflict and creates problems for us, in both personal and professional relationships. Every one of us has hidden aspects of our mental life, those that remain in our unconscious and thus outside of our awareness.

This book is about helping people to understand the psychological defense mechanisms that keep painful emotions, thoughts and fears outside of awareness. If as you read, you start to say things like: "I do that." or "That's me all over." acknowledge the feelings that are present. If the feelings take you back to something too painful for you to deal with, then seek professional help.

You wouldn't sit at home with your leg hanging off, why do it with your head falling apart. Seek out a mental health professional. They can help, but only if you ask.

1.2 Caveat

Before I continue further it would be remiss of me not to acknowledge that there are some in the field of psychology who disagree with the idea of defense mechanisms and are deeply skeptical about anything connected with the work of Sigmund Freud, the originator of the concept. As with all aspects of psychology there are differing opinions on what goes on in the human brain. That said, when we see issues arising every day that can, in many ways be explained by a theory, it is hard not to see utility in that theory. From a practical point of view, giving people a better understanding of the theory behind defense mechanisms, can help them overcome difficulties in their lives, difficulties they are likely to encounter in the real world and difficulties they may have in learning new things that are required for their work. Hopefully, in years to come neuro-scientists can give us an accurate picture of what is going on inside our brains, under any given set of circumstances. For now, let's work with what we have and what we know helps.

1.3 Why understanding is important

As we shall see later, defense mechanisms are useful, and we all need them. However, if they are over used or used inappropriately, they can cause significant problems for us. These problems are often exacerbated when we are under stress. Furthermore, it is extremely difficult to learn new things if part of our brain is screaming "No.

No. No. That is wrong." To learn something new requires us firstly to acknowledge that a change is needed in how we are perceiving something. Unfortunately, defense mechanisms can and do block our minds to new knowledge and make us resistant to changing our behavior. While defense mechanisms protect us from and help us to navigate the difficult aspects of life, they often stand in the way of growth and satisfaction.

In addition, the inappropriate use of defense mechanisms reduces the effectiveness of our emotional processing. If we are not cognizant of our personal tendencies about using defense mechanisms, they can lead us to destructive behavior. For example: People often adopt a position of denial about impending bad news without even realizing they are doing it. They won't even acknowledge the potentially negative effects let alone prepare for them. This 'head in the sand' approach works just fine, until their world comes crashing down. In other cases, people fail to recognize that the painful event they have buried in their unconscious is, adversely affecting their day-to-day behavior. This is often seen with victims of trauma who develop an obsessive need for control in every situation.

We can't eliminate the use of defense mechanisms, nor would we want. However, with greater knowledge of what they are and how they function and a greater self-awareness of how and when we employ them, we are better able to see when they are helping us and when they are hurting us.

1.4 Defense mechanisms explained

The famous psychoanalyst Sigmund Freud (1961)

first proposed defense mechanisms. Freud identified strategies that we use to protect ourselves from suffering which he called defense mechanisms. At that time, Freud used these defense mechanisms to describe and explain the abnormal behavior of his patients. Only later was the term transferred to the wider population. The definition Freud used at the time and which is still in use today is:

"A defensive mechanism developed by the ego when under pressure by the superego and external reality, which enables us to fight anxiety."

Freud explained that these defense mechanisms are extremely important to protect a person's ego, and without them, when a person encountered stressful events, they would just crumble under the pressure. Such events could cause severe mental stress and make daily living all but impossible.

A more modern definition of a defense mechanism from the Cambridge Dictionary (2018) is:

"An automatic way of behaving or thinking by which you protect yourself from something, especially from feeling unpleasant emotions."

Collins Dictionary (2018) defines it thus:

"A defense mechanism is a way of behaving or thinking which is not conscious or deliberate and is an automatic reaction to unpleasant experiences or feelings such as anxiety and fear."

Aside from being written in much clearer language the important difference in these definitions are the inclusion of the word 'automatic.' We have no conscious awareness that we are using them – It's not a deliberate decision; it happens outside of our awareness, in ways that are automatic.

Defense mechanisms are a psychological strategy that people use unconsciously to cope with what they perceive as a harmful or stressful situation and to preserve their self-image. They are part of normal everyday functioning and used appropriately they allow us to cope with disappointment, manage stress and control strong negative emotions. They can also be of use when we find ourselves encountering something, we believe to be morally unacceptable. Freud believed that defense mechanisms were necessary, but generally negative in their impact. Many agree with this view, believing that because most defense mechanisms are essentially based upon lies, and the only thing they achieve, especially if continually relied upon, is to create more problems.

There are many different defense mechanisms and though they all function in different ways their purpose is the same. When we're confronted with an idea or feeling that we find too painful we fight it off by pushing it into our unconscious mind.

Defense mechanisms are different from conscious coping strategies, in that they operate at an unconscious level, so we are unaware of their existence or how the mechanism is functioning. Another problem with defense mechanisms is that if they are used for a long time, they may become automatic and separate us from our true feelings and from reality. They subtly distort the way in which we perceive 'reality' and the way we think about ourselves. Defense mechanisms can become characteristic of how we behave, influencing our behavior over prolonged periods of time. In addition, defense mechanisms operate in the here-and-now, with no thought for tomorrow. They're unthinking and reflexive; their aim only to ward off pain at this very moment. They don't consider the long-term costs of doing so.

Cramer, one of the leading authorities on defense mechanisms identified seven key tenets of defense mechanisms which she referred to as the 'Seven Pillars' (Cramer, 2009). These seven pillars provide a clear understanding of defense mechanism theory. Cramer says of defense mechanisms:

1. They are cognitive operations that operate outside of our awareness

2. There is a chronology in their development. This is due, at least in part, to the increasing cognitive complexity of using certain mechanisms. We start using defense mechanisms as infants and as the nature of the defenses becomes more complex, we require increasingly complex cognitive functioning to use the more advanced ones.

3. They are part of normal, everyday functioning. The use of mature defenses will support successful functioning: the use of immature defenses will be related to less successful functioning. (The levels of defense mechanism are discussed in Chapter 4.)

4. Under conditions of increased stress, there will be increased reliance on defense mechanisms.

5. When we use them under conditions of stress, they will reduce the conscious experience of anxiety or other, negative affect. Cramer believed

this tenet is at the heart of defense mechanism theory as the purpose of the mechanisms is to reduce pain.

6. The use of defense mechanism will be related to other non-volitional, non-conscious processes that are associated with anxiety. Defense mechanisms are intended to reduce anxiety/pain/stress. When these conditions exist, they are accompanied by other physiological symptoms that we would normally associate with anxiety/stress. It stands to reason that if we are using a defense mechanism to combat anxiety/stress then there are going to be physiological signs that the problem is present. We would expect to find that when we are using defense mechanisms that there is also a stress induced activation of the autonomic nervous system.

7. The excessive use of defense mechanisms or the use of immature, age-inappropriate mechanisms is associated with mental illness. While defense mechanisms are intended to protect us from pain or loss of self-esteem their excessive or inappropriate use is maladaptive.

1.5 The 'id', the 'ego' and the 'super-ego'

Many people will have come across the words: 'id', 'ego' and 'super-ego' and while an in-depth knowledge of these concepts is not needed to understand defense mechanisms a brief explanation may make for a better understanding. Sigmund Freud described personality as being made up of three components: the id, the ego and the super-ego. At the time of Freud's writing (1890's) understanding of the human brain was very limited and his writing is also heavily influenced by the morals of the time. While Freud's concepts are in some ways simplistic and dated, they are useful in explaining what goes on in the brain.

1. The id. The id (Latin meaning 'It') is all about pleasure and is responsible for satisfying our bodily needs, basic instincts and animalistic drives, particularly the aggressive and sexual drives. The id is present from birth and according to Freud acts in an unconscious manner. It is the source of our libido and fuels instinctive behavior. It is all about selfish activities. It has no thought for the demands of reality. It is childish, pleasure-oriented and has no ability to delay gratification. 'I see it and I want it now.' The id is the party animal and the person you want for the road trip to Vegas.

2. The Super-ego. The super-ego contains societal and parental rules that we have internalized about what is 'good' and 'bad' and 'right' and 'wrong. The super-ego is also influenced by others who have held a similar place to that of parents such as teachers, cultural leaders and role models. As such it is constructed from our experiences in life. The super-ego aims for perfection. The super-ego acts as our moral compass, comprising of morals and values that are instilled in us. If there is too much super-ego activity, we tend to place an over reliance on defense mechanisms in order to function. It is what many of us would refer to as our 'conscience'. We don't want the super-ego on the trip to Vegas, but they

are useful to have around as a designated driver and are probably the person our parents hoped we would marry.

3. The ego. The ego (Latin meaning 'I') acts as a mediator between the impulses sought by the id and the rules imposed by the super-ego. The id and the super-ego are always in conflict and the ego balances the desires of both with what reality dictates. The ego is principally a regulating mechanism that enables us to delay gratifying immediate needs and so be able to function effectively, in the real world. The ego is about meeting long-term needs and avoiding harm. The super-ego's demands often oppose those of the id, so the ego can have a hard time in reconciling the two and to achieve this, sometimes it ends up masking reality. In some ways for the ego, it is all about doing what it needs to do just to carry on functioning in life. Finally, the ego is the part of our personality, we usually show to the world. The ego has a great time in Vegas but feels guilty about it afterwards.

Another way of explaining the id, ego and super ego is the idea of driving a horse and cart:

a) The id is the 'horse'. It tries go where it wants to go.

b) The ego is the 'driver' of the cart. The driver can guide the horse (the id), but never has full control. If the horse wants to go in a different direction from the driver, the driver is powerless to stop it.

c) The superego is the 'driver's father', telling the driver (the ego) how to manage the horse and telling him his mistakes. The father tries to keep his son, and the horse and cart on the straight and narrow. The driver may choose to listen or to ignore his father. However, if he ignores him there will be painful consequences.

There are three common scenarios where defense mechanisms are likely to be employed:

a) When the id impulses conflict with each other. For example: we may want to grab food from another person (id) but this conflicts with our desire to stay safe (id).

b) When the id impulses conflict with super-ego values and beliefs. For example: The conflict that would arise where the we desire to have sex with a stranger (id) while we know that this is contrary to societal expectations (super-ego).

c) When an external threat is posed to the ego. For example: When someone attacks our professionalism or ability we will want to protect against damage to our self-esteem (ego).

1.6 Conscious, Sub-conscious and Unconscious

Throughout this book we will refer to the 'conscious' mind and the 'unconscious' mind. However, in the interests of clarity we must first explain the meaning of the terms conscious, sub-conscious and unconscious. There is often significant confusion in the use of these words. Much of this confusion stems from Freud's original use of the words and concerns about the validity of some of his work. Here, we will provide general interpretations of the terms that suffice to aid understanding.

Explaining what is meant by the term the conscious mind is relatively easy. The conscious is the part of our mind that is responsible for our awareness of what is going on now. We are aware of both the events occurring on the outside, as well as some specific mental functions happening within us. For example, we are aware of where we are sitting, the people around us, and how we are feeling about those people. When working with your conscious mind you can form intentions and engage in introspection.

When it comes to understanding the terms sub-conscious and unconscious the task is not so easy. There is significant debate over which is the correct term to use. While unconscious is often used as a synonym for subconscious, the two terms have different meanings.

One explanation of the subconscious is that it is the part of our mind which notices and remembers information even when we are not actively trying to do so and that it influences our behavior even though we do not realize it. Our subconscious mind registers things and acquires information which our conscious mind is not aware of and it is sometimes referred to as the preconscious mind because the information stored is just below the level of consciousness. Furthermore, the subconscious consists of information that we become aware of only when we direct our attention to that information. As such, the subconscious mind is believed to contain memories that we can choose to remember. Sometimes we do not need to access this information on a conscious level. Many of us will have driven home and arrived there with no conscious memory of the actual drive – we have been seemingly running on auto-pilot.

Much of the confusion about the term unconscious stems from use of the same word in a medical context to refer to someone who has been 'knocked out' because of trauma or anesthetized prior to an operation. Unconscious is the term usually preferred by psychologists and refers to the thoughts we have that are "out of reach" of our consciousness. It is made up of countless memories and experiences we have stored in memory, throughout our lifetime, even though we cannot recall, most of those memories. The unconscious is also the dumping ground for all our memories that have been repressed or which we don't wish to, or need to, recall. These can include traumatic events in our childhood that we have blocked out, but it can also contain very trivial details like the name of a child we used to play with or the details of a trip we made as a child to visit an aged family friend. The unconscious carries all the thoughts and feelings we either find too painful to bear, or which conflict with our morality and values and that undermine our self-image. A lot of the time we may not want to know about the contents of our unconscious.

We cannot easily remember anything in our unconscious without some form of assistance. A memory can be there, but we will have great difficulty remembering it, no matter how hard we try. The memory can be triggered by something that is linked to the memory and encoded at the same time the memory was stored. This may include a song that was heard at the time of the event or a smell that was present during the event. Contained within in the unconscious are also the beliefs, ideas and attitudes that drive our lives, operating without our knowledge. Throughout the remainder of the book we will use the term conscious to refer to activity taking place in our brain which we are aware of, and unconscious to refer to activity taking place of which we are unaware. Defense mechanisms work on the unconscious level.

1.7 Abnormal use

One way of viewing defense mechanisms is that of considering them as operating on a spectrum ranging from doing what they are supposed to do (protecting us) and when they become part of a psychological disorder. To do this we have to understand a bit about what is considered abnormal and here we turn to the science of psychopathology.

Psychopathology is the study of the causes and the development of mental disorders. It includes the origin of mental disorders, how they develop, and the symptoms they might produce in a person. A person can be said to be showing signs of 'psychopathology' meaning that they appear mentally ill. When diagnosing a person with a psychological disorder a mental health professional will search for abnormalities in their behavior and often this is measured against the "norm" within the cultural context in which the person has developed. There are four indicators of abnormality, each of which is explained below:

1. Deviance. Deviance refers to a concept that the person has thoughts or behaviors that are judged unacceptable or uncommon by the cultural group to which the person belongs. It is important to note that deviance is culturally defined

and refers to a divergence from cultural/group norms or standards, most often in a social or sexual way. In short, the person is behaving contrary to what their culture expects. Deviance can sometimes be relative to a place and time. What is considered deviant in one social context may be non-deviant in another. Where deviant behavior is present it is an indicator of abnormality.

2. Distress. Psychological distress occurs when a person is behaving in a way that causes them, or others around them, to have negative feelings or emotions, to an extent that these feelings impact on their functioning in everyday life. Sadness, anxiety, depression, agitation, disturbance in sleep, loss of appetite, and having numerous aches and pains, are all manifestations of psychological distress. Distress is a subjective experience and people manifest it in different ways. Where distress is present it is an indicator of abnormality.

3. Dysfunction. Dysfunction involves any maladaptive behavior that impairs an individual's ability to perform normal daily functions and live a normal, healthy lifestyle. Maladaptive behaviors are types of behavior that keep a person from adjusting properly to situations. For example: many people with social anxiety inadvertently develop maladaptive behaviors to cope with social situations. They conceal their viewpoint and /or avoid social situations. Dysfunction can escalate to a level where the person's behavior is irregular to the extent they cannot function in daily life. Dysfunction can indicate abnormality.

4. Danger. Danger involves a pattern of functioning that is dangerous or violent and is directed at (a) the individual or (b) other people. Indications of danger to the self, include ignoring needs of diet or health, any behavior that involves carelessness, poor judgment, and any hostility that jeopardizes the person's wellbeing or that of others. Where behavior is harmful to one's self or others it is seen as abnormal.

In lay terms behavior is abnormal if:

a. It's weird.

b. It's distressing.

c. It's destructive.

d. It's dangerous.

If we feel we are at the higher end of the spectrum, to the extent that these four indicators are present and impacting on our daily life, then we should be seeking professional help. Unfortunately, it is very difficult to see where our own behavior has crossed the line of just being 'quirky', to where we have a mental health issue. The very nature of defense mechanisms renders us all but blind to the fact that we may be hurting inside. However, if others, and particularly our friends, are telling us there is a problem, then we should at least open our mind to the possibility. In a similar vein, we may notice the indicators in others, but it must always be borne in mind that:

1. For there to be concerns one needs to look at the nature of the behavior in terms of its level and consistency. If it appears more often and is more

vociferous in its nature, then this is a strong indicator something is amiss.

2. It is the job of a mental health professional to make a diagnosis and not a lay person.

3. Care and sensitivity must be used when raising the issue with a person, remembering that the person is most likely to fall back on the very defense mechanisms that are causing them problems.

1.8 Conclusion

Before continuing it is important to be clear about when there is a problem with the use of defense mechanisms. There are three indicators:

1. Inappropriate. If the person is using inappropriate and/or, immature or neurotic defense mechanisms, then there is a problem.

2. Incidence. If the person is using defense mechanisms too frequently, then there is a problem.

3. Intensity. If the person uses defense mechanisms in a particularly forceful manner, then there is a problem.

2 - LIFE HURTS

"Secrets of the heart are different. They are private and painful,
and we want nothing more than to hide them from the world.
They do not swell and press against the mouth. They live in the
heart, and the longer they are kept, the heavier they become.
It is better to have a mouthful of poison than a secret of the heart.
Any fool will spit out poison, but we hoard these painful
treasures. We swallow hard against them every day, forcing them
deep inside us. There they sit, growing heavier, festering. Given
enough time, they cannot help but crush the heart that holds
them."

The Wise Man's Fear - Patrick Rothfuss

2.1 Introduction

As we have already discussed the purpose of defense mechanisms are to avoid or minimize pain to ourselves. This pain can take many forms, some of them obvious and others hidden to us. In this chapter we will look at different types of psychological pain and provide examples of some of the ways we try to avoid it. As we will see some of our pain, and more relevantly our ways of dealing with pain can originate in our early years. As we explore the subject we can see where our defense mechanisms have been used to keep secret from our conscious mind, experiences that were too painful to deal with. Unfortunately, as alluded to in the Rothfuss' quote above, these 'secrets' have the potential to continually impact on our behavior in a negative way. Such is one of the downsides of defense mechanisms.

2.2 Pain

While the concept of physical pain is generally understood what constitutes psychological pain is less well so. There are several key points which aid in our understanding of pain in the psychological sense:

- Pain is subjective. Something that has little impact on one person may be crushing for another. One person who loses their job may say "I will get another one.", while for another person this may lead them to feelings of worthlessness and rejection.

- Pain is contextual. It depends on the circumstances that form the setting in which the person feels the hurt. What may be brushed aside under one set of circumstances becomes devasting with a change in the circumstances. For example: losing £20 may be a bit annoying if you are out socializing with friends but if you have just lost your job and need that money, you may be fraught with anguish.

- Pain is on a continuum. It can vary from minor irritation to suicide. Sometimes the pain we are feeling is distracting and at other times it can make us hurt so much it seems that the only logical solution is stepping in front of a high-speed train.

- Pain sucks. Regardless of when it occurs or in whatever form it is manifested, we don't like it and we will do whatever we need to do to avoid it.

- Pain can appeal. When a person is mentally ill, and they have effectively anesthetized themselves to the world, feeling pain, can have a perverse appeal. The rationale being: feeling pain is better than feeling nothing. The human mind can be a strange place. This desperation is well captured in the Nine Inch Nails song "Hurt":

> *'I hurt myself today*
> *To see if I still feel*
> *I focus on the pain*
> *The only thing that's real'*

Pain can originate in many ways and we have many ways of trying to describe it. The more accurately we can describe what we are feeling, the better chance we have of understanding what is happening and the better hope there is for us managing that pain correctly.

It is important to know what the common types of psychological pain look like. We will now explore some of the different ways we will experience pain.

2.3 Real Pain and Counterfeit Pain

In our attempts to understand complex psychological issues it can sometimes be useful to use analogies. To distinguish between types of pain we can use the terms 'real pain' and 'counterfeit pain'. We use these terms to draw a distinction between what would be considered as pain resulting from the everyday tribulations of life, which we refer to as 'real' pain and the neurotic/pathological interpretations of those tribulations which we will refer to as 'counterfeit' pain.

The choice of the words real and counterfeit are intended to convey the idea that one of these types comes from the healthy mind and is, an objective assessment, real given the circumstances. The other type stems from an unhealthy interpretation of events and is therefore by its nature counterfeit or fake. Consider a Rolex watch: a 'real' Rolex will stand up to scrutiny and the facts will support that it is real, whereas a counterfeit may look like a Rolex until someone starts to examine it and it becomes apparent that the parts from which it is constructed and the way in which it is constructed are fake. This is not to say that the counterfeit pain does not look and feel like the real thing, just as a counterfeit watch can tell the time. It is intended to convey that if one was to examine it closely counterfeit pain would be found to be created from flawed thinking and using poor evidence.

Real pain comes from normal human experiences, such as the death of a family member, harassment, abuse or threats, traumatic incidents, and the failures and the disappointments we all encounter at some stage in life. The break of an intimate relationship brings real pain as does the sadness encountered on losing a friend. This type of pain is normal. It is all part of the deal we call living. It comes and hopefully we deal with it, or it fades to a bearable level over time.

Counterfeit pain is pain that is unnecessary, unhealthy and damaging to us. It is unnecessary because it can be avoided. It can be considered both neurotic[1]

---

[1] A person who is neurotic tends to be emotionally unstable or unusually anxious about things that would normally be considered unimportant.

and/or pathological[2] in nature. This type of pain originates from how we interpret what we are experiencing.
In this case our interpretations are deeply flawed and the
way we are viewing events is distorted. Counterfeit pain
leads to us making negative judgements about ourselves
and having consistently negative views of the world and
our place in it. Counterfeit pain is manufactured using a
mix of subjective judgements and an inability to take on
board positive feedback. When this type of pain takes
hold of a person it can often be harder felt and longer
lasting than real pain. For some it becomes all pervasive.
This type of pain is symptomatic of a mental health problem. This type of pain is avoidable.

2.4 Childhood and the subjective response to pain

Childhood lasts a long time for human beings. The
way we live now means that a person stays in the family
home for a much longer period than is natural. It can be
argued that once a child reaches puberty then they
should be leaving the parental home and commencing to
set up an independent life. Everything physical they need
to do this is present.

Even if we set aside for the moment the way in which
childhood is prolonged, particularly in western cultures,
childhood is still a lengthy period and it is here that we
begin to learn our defense mechanisms.

Life begins with dependency. An infant cannot survive without the help of a parent. If the parents provide

---

[2] Pathological here means 'relating to mental illness.' A person's
behavior is pathological if they behave in an extreme way and have
very powerful feelings which they cannot control.

the infant with what she needs, she develops a sense of safety and security in the world. She knows that if she needs something her needs will be taken care of. If she is hungry, she will be fed. If she is in pain, she will be nursed. Love and attention are continually provided. Memories of being cared for accumulate and the infant learns that her parent/s will return again and again when she needs something. The infant grows in a secure and loving environment and this gives her emotional stability and greater confidence in dealing with problems that will arise in later life. Through seeing love the infant develops a capacity to love. Central to the development of an infant is the idea of dependency. In short, infants need someone to care for them. Having a parent/s who show empathy and provide for her needs, means she develops the ability to empathize with others and respond appropriately to meet the needs of others.

As the child grows, her development continues to rely on the parent/s to meet her evolving needs and to shape her understanding of the nature of the world. If the parent/s continue to meet these needs she will grow in a healthy well-adjusted way. If the parent/s share knowledge, provide answers and set realistic boundaries then she learns how to correctly interpret the world. If the parent/s demonstrate emotional stability, show on-going healthy interaction with others, provide the child with a role model for communicating effectively, and encourage the child to interact with both other children and adults then she will be able to engage effectively with whoever she meets later in life. If the parent/s reveal their emotions, this will encourage the child to become emotionally competent.

We are not talking about some sort of 'perfect parenting', for that does not exist. What we are referring to is parenting that is sufficient to meet the physical and psychological needs of the child. If the parenting is 'good enough', that's good enough.

Contrast this with the parent who shows a lack of love and doesn't provide for the infant's needs. If the infant grows in a world where food is not brought when he is hungry, where emotional support he needs is not present, and where his pain is not attended to, then instead of feeling safe and secure the infant learns only fear and pain. The fear and pain become unbearable, and the infant has no capacity to understand or deal with what is happening. He must find a way to deal with it and the only option available for him is to mask his awareness of it. This is where he begins to use defense mechanisms. And it is here that those defense mechanisms become imbedded in a relationship with intolerable pain. While the infant has no conscious memory of this, memories and the associated links are deeply ingrained in their psyche. If his needs aren't met during the first couple of years of life, when he is completely helpless, this shapes his capacity to trust and rely on others in later years. The first two years of life are a critical time-period for mental development. After two years, abnormal brain developments remain, and the person can never make up for inadequate parenting during this period.

As if that was not bad enough, imagine now, this child growing in a home where violence and chaos abound. At best he gets enough food to aid in his physical development but the essentials for a healthy mental development are absent. His parent/s may have limited, if any, parenting skills. His parent/s may provide little in terms of socialization and may be emotionally distant. One or both of his parents may be absent, leaving him to be raised by a distant relative or in a children's home. If he has no one there to protect him, he will place a greater reliance on his defense mechanisms to hide or minimize the pain.

When this child reaches adulthood and manages to escape the parental home, he is likely to find little support in the wider world and so place an even greater need to rely on the defenses he has. Alternatively, he may feel unable to escape and stay with a controlling parent, because he has learned to be fearful of the outside world. At least, in that 'home' world, he knows he has developed defenses to help him deal with the reality that is there.

We can see how the way each of these children has been brought up is likely to have a significant impact on the way that they deal with the stresses of life. The girl from the emotional stable and giving home is more likely to have an emotionally secure foundation to deal with stress while the boy is much more likely to overly use the defense mechanisms he has developed throughout childhood, defense mechanisms that are not fit for purpose.

Although these are two simplistic examples of the way in which we deal with pain as children, and of how defense mechanisms evolve under different circumstances, they illustrate the means by which, when we are subjected to stressful/fearful situations the amount of pain and how we deal with it becomes subjective.

Perhaps the saddest thing about this type of pain is its longevity. Pain from childhood can be extremely hard to shift. These types of wounds seem to be able to hurt us all over again with the slightest of excuses. As George R.R. Martin, says in his book, A Game of Thrones:

> *"Some old wounds never truly heal, and bleed again at the slightest word."*

2.5 Self-image

Most people have a preferred image of themselves. Most of the time, this self-image is inaccurate and more favorable to the person than would result from an objective assessment by another person. Our self-image is very important and as such we will do whatever needs doing, to sustain it. To do this, we continually deceive ourselves. These self-deceptions are often so small in nature and occur so frequently that we do not even realize they are happening.

However, when an internal or external event occurs that is clearly at odds with our self-image this creates a conflict for us. Such an internal conflict causes us pain. The level of pain formed can vary from mild annoyance to a crisis in confidence. For example: I believe I am a very intelligent person. Someone explains something to me, and I can't understand it. This makes me feel stupid and challenges my self-image of being high in intelligence. To protect my self-image, I tell myself that the thing was 'poorly explained' or 'not important'. By doing so I protect the belief I hold, that I am high in intelligence. In short, if our self-image feels under threat there is psychological pain. As with any pain we need to have some way to defend our self-image against this threat and our default setting is often our defense mechanisms.

2.6 Anxiety

Anxiety is a feeling of unease, that can be mild or severe. Everyone has feelings of anxiety at some point in their life. For example: we may feel anxious about sitting an exam, a job interview or a medical test. These feelings are perfectly normal. The primary function of anxiety is believed to be that of acting as a 'signal' to warn us of a threat to our equilibrium, or of impending danger. As such, anxiety may be a crucial tool which helps us to survive.

However, when anxiety levels are heightened or prolonged it creates a very unpleasant feeling of apprehensiveness. Symptoms of anxiety can range in number, intensity, and frequency, depending on the person. It is often characterized by physical manifestations because of activity within the autonomic nervous system, typically including sensations of heat and cold all over the body and shaking or jitteriness. These symptoms will often be accompanied by nervous behavior, such as pacing back and forth, somatic complaints, and rumination about the past.

Unfortunately, anxiety is self-perpetuating. Of those suffering from it, many often have poor social skills and may be inflexible in problem solving, have an inability to focus and engage in high levels of impulsive behavior. Cognitive distortions (discussed in chapter 4) such as overgeneralizing, and catastrophizing, can lead to anxiety. For example: an overgeneralized belief that something bad will "always" happen can lead someone to be overly stressed of even minimally risky situations. Chronic anxiety occurs when there are prolonged daily symptoms that reduce the quality of the person's life, or it can be experienced through sporadic, stressful panic attacks known as acute anxiety.

2.7 Fear

Fear is a reaction to real external dangers. It is an unpleasant emotion caused by the perceived threat of danger, pain, or harm. It causes a change in metabolic and organ functions and ultimately a change in behavior. Fear is there to help us avoid harm. It can be controlled by the process of cognition and learning. For example: Fear can be learned by experiencing or watching a frightening traumatic incident. It can also be affected by cultural influences and the context in which it occurs. For example: If there is a lot of media attention in relation to knife attacks, we are more likely to be fearful of such an attack happening to us. This type of fear messaging can be very powerful, as it acts on our unconscious and gets us to do things we have not really thought through. A significant amount of advertising, particularly in North America, works on fear messaging.

Fear can be separated into two categories:

1. The fear which is rational or appropriate for the circumstances. For example: A person standing at the edge of a high cliff is perfectly rational in their fear of falling off the cliff because of the high likelihood of death if they did fall.

2. The fear that is irrational or inappropriate. An irrational fear that persists is called a phobia. For example: A person who suffers from arachnophobia is frightened of spiders. This can be viewed as irrational given the size of a human and

the size of the spider.

Fear can be differentiated from anxiety in four ways:

1. The duration of emotional experience. Fear is generally short-lived whereas anxiety is long acting.

2. The temporal focus. Fear is focused on the present, whereas anxiety is focused on the future.

3. The specificity of the threat. Fear is geared towards a specific threat, whereas the focus of anxiety is towards a more general or diffuse perception of threat.

4. The motivated direction. Fear is about escaping from the threat by whatever means possible, whereas anxiety leads to excessive attention towards a potential threat and so interferes with coping with that threat.

As can be seen from these differences, anxiety is in effect about a state of mind, as opposed to fear, which is functional and geared to survival. In short, anxiety is about worrying about a threat while fear is about motivating us to do something about the threat.

2.8 Cognitive dissonance

While there are many circumstances in which we are likely to use defense mechanism one of the times we are most likely to see defense mechanisms at play is when there is cognitive dissonance. Leon Festinger (1957) developed a theory in which he highlighted the fact that where a person's actions are contrary to their values or beliefs, an internal conflict is created for the person.

Festinger called this internal conflict 'cognitive dissonance'. When cognitive dissonance is at play, the person's mind will be in an uncomfortable state. Depending on the extent of the conflict, the dissonance can vary from a mild irritation to something that is all consuming. Our actions influence our beliefs.

There are three parts to cognitive dissonance theory:

1. People do not like it when there is inconsistency between their actions and their values. We all have a set of values, made up of our attitudes and beliefs. These values emerge as we go through life and are created by a combination of our personality, the people we have around us, live events and our ability to correctly interpret those events. Figure 2.1 illustrates how our value system emerges. Although our values can change, change often requires the acceptance of new knowledge or a significant event in our life. For the most part, our values are enduring and resilient.

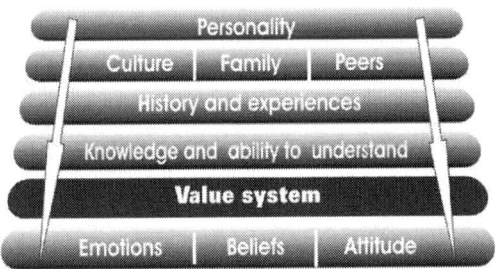

Figure 2.1: A Value System.

Each person likes to act in a way that is consistent with their values. If we do something that conflicts with our values, we notice the conflict, and we start to get an uncomfortable feeling. Identifying the conflict can take place on an unconscious level and if this is the case, we may refer to it as having a 'nagging doubt.' At other times we may hear someone say: "I just felt bad about it." They can recognize that something is amiss but can't put their finger on what is causing their discomfort. Examples of cognitive dissonance are many. We promise a friend to help them paint a room in their house. On the day of the job we are tired and make an excuse that we are sick and can't do it. This leads to us feeling bad all day, and even for many days' afterward. What has happened is this: Our values say we have made a promise so we should keep it, but our actions meant that we broke your promise. The way we acted (breaking the promise) was inconsistent with our values (we should always keep a promise) and dissonance is created.

2. When a person recognizes dissonance is present, they will be motivated to do something to resolve that dissonance. Most people do not know exactly what is going on in their mind, but they will know if they don't like how they feel. And they will want a bad feeling to go away. The greater the dissonance is, the stronger the motivation will be to do something about it. It must be remembered that the strength of the dissonance cannot be underestimated. The level of dissonance we feel is subjective, and often exacerbated by circumstances. Cognitive dissonance can bring on some strong emotional reactions. If we consider the example above of us breaking our promise to paint the friend's house: How much worse are we going to feel if our friend,

then says: "Don't worry about the painting. You are sick and that is much more important. I will come around and look after you." Now we have broken our promise and we did it with someone who really cares for us. The dissonance increases. In our brain we begin to search for a way to make the bad feeling go away.

3. The cognitive dissonance can be resolved using three methods. On recognizing that cognitive dissonance is present and being motivated to remove it, there are three strategies we can adopt to address the problem:

a) Change our values. One might think that changing our values would be the simplest way to resolve the dissonance. Considering our example above we could say: "I no longer believe I must keep a promise." In theory this would resolve the conflict. If we don't believe in keeping promises, there is no conflict when we break a promise, so the dissonance is resolved. However, as we pointed out earlier our values are generally consistent and resistant to change. We rely on our values to make sense of the world. While changing our values may appear a simple option, we are very unlikely to use this method.

b) Change our actions. An easy option would appear to be that of changing our actions; in other words, not doing the thing that conflicts with our values. There are two main problems with this option. First, we may want to do the thing. For example: My values may say that it is wrong to have an affair but here is a very attractive person with whom I want to have an intimate relationship. If I let my values dictate my actions and don't go ahead with the illicit affair, then I am now going to feel bad about not getting what I wanted. It's a no-win situation. The second problem with changing our actions is that often we have already done the thing that conflicts with our values. It seemed like a good idea at the time, and our desire/need took charge and we acted. Now our values are back in charge and there is a huge conflict bouncing in our head.

c) Change our perception of the actions. A third and more complex method of resolving the dissonance is to change the way we perceive our action. If we choose this option, we distort reality, changing how we view the action, or we chose to remember it in a way that is more acceptable to us. Most of us will remember the American president who "did not have sexual relationships with that woman". Here the distortion revolved around the meaning of the words: sexual relationships. In saying he did not have 'sexual relationships' he was taken to mean he did not have sexual intercourse. He did have oral sex. While undoubtedly in this case a lot of the behavior was driven by political expedience, we can see how a person could distort reality in a similar way to ease their cognitive dissonance. "I did not have sexual intercourse. I only had oral sex and that doesn't count." My actions and values are not in conflict. Matter resolved. Isn't it great how the brain works!

Cognitive dissonance is an aspect of our daily lives. While managing it becomes second nature for us, we do not always do it in an appropriate way.

2.9 Embarrassment

Embarrassment is an emotional state which we experience when we do something, we believe to be socially unacceptable and it is witnessed by, or revealed to, others. Embarrassment can also be as a result of us being exposed doing something that we would consider to be a private matter, such as being caught naked, being seen using the toilet, or being interrupted in a sexual act. Farting in public in some cultures, particularly when members of the opposite sex are present, can be very embarrassing, even though everyone does it. We can also be embarrassed if we make a mistake, especially if it is highlighted by someone and if the incident is related to our work. Being caught out in a lie is another common source of embarrassment. It does not have to be something we have done that makes us embarrassed. We can also be embarrassed by the actions of someone who is seen as being closely associated with us. For example: A family member or work colleague. It is usually easy to detect when someone has been embarrassed as there are likely to be strong non-verbal indicators, such as blushing, gaze aversion and fidgeting. Often, we will try and cover up our embarrassment with a joke or a nervous laugh. In most circumstances the feeling of embarrassment is neither severe nor long-term. However, sometimes depending on the nature of the incident, the context in which it occurs and the person whom it affects, embarrassment can have a significant impact. Culture can also play a significant part in the level of embarrassment felt.

2.10 Guilt and Shame

Moving on from embarrassment we find two other related aspects - guilt and guilt's cousin, the one we metaphorically hide in the woodshed - shame. [Why we are much more prone to keep shame hidden will become apparent.]

Guilt and shame, while similar to each other, are not the same and there is often confusion when discussing the two. The Oxford Dictionary (2018a) defines guilt as:

'A feeling of having committed wrong or failed in an obligation.'

Guilt occurs as a result of us making a comparison between what we have done in a situation and one of two things:

1.   Our standards.
2.   The ideal social standard for the prevailing context.

Where there is a significant shortfall between our actions and our own standards or, the standard expected by others in those circumstances, guilt is likely to result.

The Oxford Dictionary (2018b) defines shame as:

'A painful feeling of humiliation or distress caused by the consciousness of wrong or foolish behavior.'

Shame can often be the result of a traumatic childhood. At a time when the child is, completely dependent on their parents, how those parents behave, can lead to long-term feelings of shame. For example:

- If a child has been called 'worthless', 'ugly', 'dirty' and similar invectives, and subjected to this type of abuse from a young age, they are very likely to carry this self-image with them, into adult life and with it, a continual sense of shame relating to their existence.

- If the child is neglected and there is a lack of enough parental availability, this may be interpreted by a child to mean: "I'm not worthy of love and attention." In turn this leads to feelings of shame and an inability to form and maintain healthy relationships in later life. Often the adult may crave any attention and become involved in unhealthy relationships because they are "not worthy" of better ones.

- If a child is subjected to physical, sexual or emotional abuse this is likely to lead to a profound and long-lasting sense of shame. They will often blame themselves for provoking the abuse or feel ashamed because they did nothing to stop it. (Reality makes little difference in the mind of the child.) The accompanying loss of dignity and innocence exacerbates the sense of shame. Exposing what has happened can often lead to an increased level in the sense of shame.

Children raised in these circumstances are highly likely to rely heavily on inappropriate defense mechanisms throughout life. They are also very likely as adults to abuse drugs or alcohol and accept abusive behavior from others. Many adult victims of domestic violence were abused as children and many victims of childhood abuse are also likely to become abusers themselves. Such is the power of shame.

Shame can also stem from events in adult life:

- Where our efforts or ideas are belittled by others, particularly by those we hold in high esteem, shame is likely to result.

- Many soldiers returning from war feel a deep sense of shame about what they saw and did. Dismissing the reality that what happens in the fugue of battle bears little resemblance to everyday life, they turn these feelings inward into shame.

- Victims of sexual assault often feel a sense of shame. They may blame themselves for the way they were dressed or where they were at the time of the attack. This is often exacerbated as the assailant seeks to transfer the blame to the victim. Often, commonly held views in society don't help.

- In collectivist cultures, shame is not only experienced by the individual but the whole family, tribe or culture. So called 'honor-based' violence is an attempt at restoration for this shame to the extended group.

Analyzing the difference between shame and guilt can lead to a better understanding of the two (Tangney, 1995):

- Guilt is a less painful experience than shame because the object of disapproval with guilt, is a specific act we have done, whereas shame is about disapproval of us, in our entirety.

- The cognitive content of guilt is focused on our particular actions only and can be summed up with the phrase: "I have done a bad thing", while the cognitive content of shame focuses on the self and can be summed up by the phrase: 'I am bad.' Fossum and Mason (1986, p5) write: "While guilt is a painful feeling of regret and responsibility for one's actions, shame is a painful feeling about oneself as a person."

- When we feel guilty, we are more likely to adopt a social approach response. Our inclination will be to fix the situation, to compensate those harmed and to make reparation. [Here, sits well the societal concept of restorative justice following conviction for a crime.] Alternatively, guilt may also lead us to adopt a hostile or aggressive approach to those confronting us regarding the act. However, shame is more likely to provoke a social avoidance, approach. We don't want others to know about our feelings of inferiority and loneliness. We don't want others to see how bad a person we truly are. Shame leads us to withdraw socially, to hide in the woodshed away from prying eyes.

- Shame makes us feel exposed. We do not need someone to have seen the cause of our shame, our imaginations are enough to create a devastating picture of how others would view us. An often-heard expression when someone feels ashamed is: "I just wanted to die...", a reference to wanting to be totally removed, forever, from what they have just done or what has been done to them. Guilt, in contrast, is typically a less devastating experience because the object of condemnation is a specific behavior, not us, as a whole, as our core identity or self-concept are not at stake.

- People who experience feelings of shame about themselves are more vulnerable to a range of psychological symptoms. Shame often makes us feel very small and leaves us with a sense of worthlessness or powerlessness.
- Shame is a very painful, social emotion and one which can last for a significant period.

The actor Mickey Rourke has spoken of how he compensated for his feelings of shame:

"I come from a violent background. So, I became hard. I realized that I had made myself that way to deal with a feeling of abandonment and shame."

How often have we seen someone lash out in what we think is in an inappropriate way given the circumstances, while at the same time we suspect that they are covering up for their own insecurity. Often the issue is more serious, and the behavior is a way for them to cover up something they are ashamed about.

2.11 Sadness

Sadness is an emotional pain typically characterized by, feelings of loss, despair, helplessness, disappointment and sorrow. With sadness we hold the feelings within us, as opposed to expressing them. We bottle-up our feelings of grief or disappointment. We are all familiar with the expression: 'Choking back the tears…' and this epitomizes the idea of sadness. It takes a lot of energy to hold emotions in check and this can leave us feeling drained to such an extent we feel physical ill (See: somatization, in Chapter 3). We may also become quiet, or lethargic, or withdraw from others. Chronic sadness is often looked upon as depression or as a precursor to depression.

2.12 Hate

Many would not consider hate as a form of pain but if we examine it from that perspective, we can see where pain and hate are at least kissing cousins. If we consider the Penguin Dictionary of Psychology (Reber and Reber, 2002) definition of hate we see hate defined as a:

"deep, enduring, intense emotion expressing animosity, anger, and hostility towards a person, group, or object."

Anything that is negative in its nature and affects us in a deep and enduring way emotionally, is not going to be pleasant for us to carry around. Furthermore, from a social perspective hate is almost universally regarded as a negative emotion with judgement being passed on the hater. Even when the hate can be justified, it is still seen as negative. This means that cognitive dissonance is often created for the person who feels hate: 'I hate, but hate is a bad thing. Therefore, I must be a bad person.' And so, the unpleasant feeling is created, for the person.

Hate is often based in a sense of perceived threat and we use acts of hate as an attempt to free ourselves from feelings of fear, injustice or helplessness. As an even simpler motive: we often hate something that is different from us. This stems from fear.

Hate can also be directed inwardly and as such creates an extremely unpleasant feeling. Often this is as a result of feelings of inadequacy or worthlessness. In a similar vein we often hate traits in people that we see in ourselves: 'I hate him. He is so selfish.' In reality, we have seen the selfishness in ourselves and project it to another.

Hate can also be used to mask pain or distract us from it. If we have lost a relative as a result of a drunk driver, we may distract ourselves from the pain of loss by directing hatred to the perpetrator and seeking punishment for him, thus avoiding being overwhelmed by the loss. Therefore, when some has died as a result of a tragedy relatives will be relentless in seeking someone to blame. As the writer James Baldwin (1964) puts it:

"I imagine one of the reasons people cling to their hates so stubbornly is because they sense, once hate is gone, they will be forced to deal with pain."

2.13 Frustration

When one mentions the word 'frustration' it may not occur to think of it in terms of hurt, but frustration is something that causes us emotional pain and anxiety. Frustration is a common emotional response which arises when we perceive that our needs, wants, or goals are being hindered or blocked. The more we perceive that our goals are being hindered or blocked the more frustrated we will become. There are two types of frustration; internal and external. Internal frustration arises when we have difficulty in fulfilling our needs or personal desires and we blame ourselves for this. Internal frustration can also arise when we have difficulty overcoming what we think of as deficiencies in our character.

This would include examples such as an inability to overcome our lack of confidence or to develop and maintain an intimate relationship. Frustration may be present because we don't know how to fix these aspects or because we are trying and failing. Either way, we get frustrated with ourselves and become annoyed and irritable.

External frustration arises when we perceive that another person is hindering or blocking us from achieving our needs, wants or goals. It can be as simple as people pushing in line in front of us, or a shop assistant who doesn't seem to grasp what exactly we want. Where we are unable to address the frustration, it will often lead to anger.

People have different levels of tolerance towards frustration. If we have a low frustration tolerance level, we will become frustrated much more easily and rapidly and are more likely to lash out at the perceived cause of the frustration. If we have a high frustration tolerance level, we will have lower levels of anger and an ability to work for longer times on more difficult tasks.

2.14 Loss

Loss is the fact of or the process of losing someone or something. It is one of the most painful emotions often leading to a sense of emptiness and ambivalence about the future. Loss is a normal reaction to an abnormal event. Because what we have lost has been an intricate part of our life, there are often reminders of that loss everywhere we go. We may imagine seeing the person's face in the crowd, we may smell the scent they wore, or we may come across an old photograph that reminds us of the time that has past.

There are many types of loss including loss of:

- Life.
- Health.
- Property of material worth.
- Property of sentimental worth.
- Status.
- Hope.
- Trust.

All of these will affect us in different ways and for different durations. We may get over a financial loss more quickly compared to the loss of a spouse, from which we may never get over. Loss can often lead to other mental health conditions such as depression or thoughts of suicide. Furthermore, if we blame someone for the loss, we are likely to be angry with them and spend considerable time seeking redress or revenge, thus perpetuating the feelings of loss.

When we have suffered a loss, we may spend considerable amount of time feeling sad, isolating ourselves from others and being reduced to tears with minimal provocation. A song on the radio or the mere mention of the person's name may lead us into floods of tears.

After some time, we may be able to come to terms with the loss and move on with our life. Accepting the loss allows us a form of closure. However, this may be easier said than done. We may not be able to accept what happened, continually reliving it and continuing to grieve for it.

2.15 Failure

Life is a series of ups and downs. We win some and we lose some. We should be able to accept this. But if we have set a goal for ourselves and we don't reach that goal, our self-esteem will suffer, and the pain is likely to set in. The more we had invested in obtaining the goal and the more importance we had placed upon it, the greater the pain will be. Often there can be significant amount of social stigma attached to failing. When a marriage breaks down, we are often more concerned about what every-one else will think about us, rather than what is happening for those immediately involved. How familiar are we with terms such as: "Her marriage failed." and how big a battering is that for our self-esteem?

2.16 Loneliness

Significant pain can stem from loneliness. Human beings are in essence 'herd animals.' We are meant to survive in groups. We need the company of others to assure us of our psychological and our physical well-being. If we are continually alone it is likely that we will spiral into a state of anxiety and depression. Where people are alone, they will often resort to unhealthy and self-defeating attitudes about their solitude. Comments such as: "I am better off on my own. People only let you down." and "You can't trust anyone." proliferate. The situation becomes self-perpetuating with pain and anxiety increasing.

Often the origin of this behavior can be traced back to earlier life when the person suffered rejection at the hands of another, a lover or a parent. However, such rejection does not need to have been a major event. If the person was of an introverted and fragile nature to start with, a simple unintended slight can be enough to start the downward spiral. Perhaps a friend forgot to call after promising to do so, or we were missed out when it came to invites for a work function. These are interpreted as deliberate snubs to which we reply in kind. Often rejection raises questions of self-worth and causes a person to adopt a negative self-image. How many of us are familiar with the proverbial 'cat lady', a cliché for someone who has isolated them self from society and sought solace with their cats. "I have my cats for company. I don't need anyone."[3]

It would be an oversight to fail to mention that a person can be lonely, even if they are in regular contact with others. Often, if we only cast a superficial glance at a person, we may think they have regular human interaction but when we look in greater depth, we can see that the person is trapped in a lifestyle where relationships are at best faux and at worst, mask an existence of isolation and suffering. For example: Consider the person trapped in an abusive relationship where no one knows the true nature of that relationship or the case of a person who is the life and soul of the office but spends their evenings alone drinking in a bar. And how often have we seen a person obsessing over every detail of a movie star or becoming immersed in a television soap opera identifying with the characters as if they knew them. The pain is there. Some of us just mask it better.

Lack of human contact is painful and by its very nature excludes one thing that is likely to alleviate that pain

---

[3] Do please excuse any typos. The cat keeps climbing on the keyboard.

– contact with others.

2.17 Numbness

Emotional numbness can be difficult to explain if you have no personal experience of it. It is often described as feeling empty or despondent. It makes some people feel isolated or leaves them with a feeling that they have no future. Some indicators that a person is emotionally numb include:

- Self-isolation – the person avoids social contact.
- Over-reaction or no reaction to an event – the person either overreacts to an event or does not react at all.
- Trouble hearing and processing everyday life – the person appears to be unable to process events that are going on around them. In many cases they will appear to just 'zone out' or will have trouble interpreting social cues.
- A failure to laugh out loud – the person cannot seem to muster enough interest to laugh aloud. At best, they may force a smile.
- A lack of desire to date or engage in a relationship.
- Excessive sleeping.

Perhaps the best-known cultural reference that alludes to the feeling to this condition is the Pink Floyd song 'Comfortably Numb':

> *"Now I've got that feeling once again*
> *I can't explain, you would not understand*
> *This is not how I am*

I have become comfortably numb."

2.18 I'm fine.

This chapter has discussed some of the ways that we feel psychological pain. It would be surprising if at least some of it hasn't struck a chord. However, for some hiding pain has become a way of life. We will only be able to identify that another is in pain if we listen carefully to what is said and how it is said. For now, let us consider a simple example. Imagine we are dealing with an emotional situation and when asked how the person is feeling they reply: "I'm fine." You can choose how you want to reply but for me the standard retort to this answer is "No, you're f**king not." Fine is a word we use to mask true feelings. When we are talking about emotion, it is us saying: 'I am hurting all over and if you can't realize that then you are no use to me. So just go away." And unfortunately, most of the time we do just that, happy to escape having to listen to someone else's pain.

2.19 Conclusion

Now we are aware of some of the ways psychological pain can affect us, it is not surprising that we, as humans, have sought numerous ways to protect ourselves from it. And having seen how much pain there is out there, and the many different ways it can hit us, we obviously are going to need a lot of tools in our psychological toolbox. In the next chapter we will look at one of the groups of tools we have at our disposal and the ones that are the primary focus of this book: defense mechanisms. Remember if we are hurting psychologically, our first resort will be to use a defense mechanism.

3 - DEFENSE MECHANISMS

*"Numbing the pain for a while will make it worse
when you finally feel it."*

Harry Potter and the Goblet of Fire - J.K. Rowling

*"People are afraid of themselves, of their own reality;
their feelings most of all."*

Jim Morrison (1943 -1971)

3.1 Introduction

In this chapter we are going to explore the different defense mechanisms. There is no consensus on the number of defense mechanisms nor is each mechanism clearly defined. Included here are the ones that we are most likely to encounter. From a theoretical standpoint there are different interpretations of what constitutes each defense mechanism and there can be significant crossover between various mechanisms. Furthermore, there is also crossover with and linkage to, other psychological concepts. Where the existence of such concepts is likely to create confusion for the reader, explanation of the linked concept is included. Having said all that one has to acknowledge that it is all very difficult for the anyone encountering defense mechanisms for the first time, to get a clear understanding of them and to draw lines of separation between some of them. What we have attempted to do here is to provide a comprehensive list of the defense mechanisms and as clear a description of them as possible. Inevitably there is overlap.

3.2 Defense mechanisms - An alphabetical List

To try and make it simpler, the defense mechanisms have initially been listed in alphabetical order. Later, we will discuss how researchers have placed mechanisms into identified groups or levels. This grouping can provide greater understanding of them and can provide greater utility for those encountering them.

Read through each mechanism a couple of times, so the concept becomes clear. With some defenses, differing explanations of the concept are given consecutively, at the beginning of their description. This is because changing nuance in the explanation can make it clearer. Thinking about when and how we may have used the defense mechanism in question, will help with understanding. Examples of each have been provided to help with clarification and to show how the inappropriate use of defense mechanisms can have a profound and long-term impact on a person.

Sometimes an adjective will be added to the name of the mechanism. This descriptor is a strong indicator of a more extreme application of that defense mechanism, often inferring that the person using this type of mechanism has serious mental health issues. We mention these variations here only to avoid confusion if a reference to them is encountered elsewhere. A total of 31 defense mechanisms are listed:

1. **Acting Out**. *Concept:* Acting out occurs when we substitute an extreme behavior in place of a normal one, to express our thoughts or feelings. We do this because we feel unable to express our thoughts in the normal way. This feeling of inability is sometimes

due to the circumstances or it is because of how we feel about ourselves. The benefit for the person in acting out is that it can release inner tension, thus allowing them to feel calmer about the exigent circumstances. However, the obvious disadvantage of this type of behavior is that it brings the person that is 'acting out', under the negative attention of others and is likely to evoke adverse commentary from them. This can damage relationships or provoke negative internal feelings for the person.

Examples:

a) Angus, a seven-year old, on a visit to the supermarket is told he is not allowed sweets. He promptly throws a tantrum, screaming at his mother and crying loudly.

b) While attending a board meeting at his place of work Maxwell feels his views are constantly being ignored by the other participants. In frustration he slams his file down on the table and storms out of the room shouting words to the effect of: "If no one is going to listen to me, I'm leaving." And for a more dramatic effect he slams the door on his way out.

c) Elizabeth, suffering from continuing mental health problems, self-harms. Injuring herself in a physical way allows her to 'act out' the internal emotional pain she is struggling to cope with.

2. **Altruism.** *Concept:* While altruism is often regarded as a virtuous trait defensive altruism, refers to an altruistic act in which there is an unconscious self-serving motivation underneath our conscious altruistic

intention. Both the degree of the self-serving motivation behind our acts and the level of our awareness of it can vary considerably. We won't want to admit, even to ourselves, that our good acts are really being done for a self-serving motive. Sometimes our altruistic behavior can reach pathological level, and it then causes us serious problems.

Where we use altruism to cope with our emotional problems or our anxiety issues, and rather than addressing our needs we channel all our energy into addressing the needs of someone else, over the long-term this will have a detrimental effect on our well-being. We may receive some form of gratification from our actions in the short-term, but this merely masks our underlying issues. While we can receive gratification from the response of others, the neglect of our own needs has an obviously detrimental effect on our life.

Altruism is a mature defense mechanism (See: chapter 4) and as such is, in most cases, likely to be more beneficial than harmful.

A more extreme version of altruisms is referred to as altruistic surrender. Altruistic surrender (Moze, 2007) is a pathological version of empathy and occurs when we internalize the values of another person and live our life in accordance with those values. We fail to recognize normal boundaries, hoping to avoid anxiety by living vicariously. We abandon our own ambitions and replaces them with someone else's.

Examples:

a) Ahmed who grew up in an abusive home is now a self-made millionaire. He donates huge sums of money to charitable foundations for victims of domestic violence but claims this has nothing to do with his own upbringing, refusing to acknowledge the impact that had on him as a child.

b) As a child, Rosemary expressed the desire to have both a career and children. While her career has been successful, she is saddened by the fact she never had children. To minimize the anxiety this causes her, she spends considerable time and money on her nephews and nieces.

3. **Anticipation.** *Concept:* Anticipation is a mechanism we use to reduce inner discomfort about things that are likely to occur in the future. Through careful planning, we can reduce the stress about a future challenge by the realistic anticipation of potential outcomes and preparation for those outcomes. Anticipation involves both thinking and feeling about the future. In some cases, all we may have to do is rehearse potential outcomes in our mind while in others it may take significant planning. As with altruism, we often use anticipation in a conscious manner. It is regarded as a mature defense mechanism but may also be regarded as a coping strategy (See: chapter 5)

However, when our emotions become highly aroused, anticipation becomes an involuntary defense mechanism. If we overly estimate the size of the problem we may have to face, we can become mentally incapacitated. The key to the effective use of anticipation is objectivity.

Example:

    a) Margery has a phobia about the dentist. Prior to her appointment she takes a few minutes to remind herself she has been to the dentist many times before with no adverse effects. This anticipation of what will happen is enough to calm her nerves.

4. **Avoidance.** *Concept:* One of the simplest defense mechanisms we can employ is that of avoidance. When we perceive a situation that is likely to create harm or anxiety for us, we simply avoid the situation. Often a person who becomes anxious in a crowded situation avoids putting themselves into a crowded place. This action is unconscious and exacerbated by them avoiding discussing the matter and how they feel about it. It can progress to a stage where they avoid thinking about the topic. Leaving the matter unresolved is a preferred option than confronting the matter. Many of us engage in avoiding situations or tasks that give us stress. Consider how many times we have avoided an awkward manager/employee conversation because we were fretful about it. We put it off to the next day, then the next, while all the time we grow more stressed about it. We put the problem in the famous "too difficult to deal with tray." The detrimental effect of avoidance can be significant as the person seeks to avoid more and more situations, perceiving them likely to be harmful.

Example:

a) Yolanda was lost as a child in a crowded shopping center. Since then, she does not like going anywhere crowded, so she avoids doing so, making excuses not to go when asked to do so by friends or family.

5. **Compartmentalization.** Concept: When we separate parts of us, from the awareness of other parts, this is referred to as compartmentalization. Compartmentalization is a lesser form of dissociation (see below). As these different parts have different values, compartmentalization allows them to co-exist by inhibiting our conscious acknowledgement of them. In creating this separation, we can avoid the cognitive dissonance that may arise by keeping our conflicting values out of our conscious mind.

Examples:

a) Henry is ruthless in his business dealings and has no issues in firing members of staff when it is financially beneficial to do so. This conflicts with his desire to appear kind and heroic to his children. He compartmentalizes the 'work Henry' and the 'home Henry' holding two separate views of himself. This reduces the potential for cognitive dissonance.

b) Bart is an elder in his church. However, when it comes to filling in his tax return, he is less than honest about his earnings. He may tell himself that the government is not using his taxes in a Christian way so justifying why he is giving less to the government. Compartmentalizing these two conflicting aspects of his life allows him to escape the obvious tension between his religious values and his actions regarding the tax return.

6. **Compensation.** *Concept:* Compensation is a process of psychologically counterbalancing perceived weaknesses by emphasizing strength in other areas. Compensation involves developing positive self-concepts to make up for and to mask perceived negative self-concepts. When we emphasize strengths, we recognize that we cannot be strong in every way and in all areas of our lives. For example: "I may not know how to cook, but I'm brilliant at cleaning up." When done appropriately and not to overcompensate, compensation helps reinforce a person's self-esteem and self-image. It can allow a person to overcome weakness and achieve success.

There are, however, unhealthy ways to compensate, such as a person who feels unloved or ugly becomes promiscuous, taking many partners thus proving they are loved and attractive. Another common aspect of compensation we are likely to recognize is referred to as 'short man syndrome' or a having 'Napoleon complex". It refers to a person who is short in stature and over compensates by overly-aggressive or domineering social behavior. The syndrome or complex carries the implication that such behavior is compensatory for the person's short stature. In a similar vein is the social stereotype of the 'jolly fat girl'. In this case the girl, conscious of herself being over-weight and believing herself to be unattractive because of this, overcompensates by always wanting to be the focus of attention in a social environment.

Examples:

a) Sarb is the only non-white child at his high school. In his mind he believes everyone is judging him on the color of his skin and so pushes himself in every aspect of the curriculum, to be the best. This behavior continues into later life where he can never find satisfaction with what he has achieved.

7. **Denial.** *Concept:* Denial is used in a situation in which a person who is faced with a fact that is too uncomfortable or painful to accept, just rejects that fact. Often the person will instead insist that the fact is not true, regardless of what may be overwhelming evidence to the contrary. Denial is an easy defense to understand and can be considered a generic defense mechanism, as it underlies many of the others. When we use denial, we simply refuse to accept the truth or reality of a fact or experience. Denial is often seen when someone is confronted with the likelihood of their own death or the death of a close relative. The pain associated with such an event is just too much to bear and their first resort is to deny the reality. A parent when confronted by the sudden death of a child may first say: "No, it can't be him. He is at school."

Denial, for a period, can help by isolating us from the full impact of a traumatic situation, allowing time to work its magic, and for us to become accustomed to what has happened.

Denial is a major cause for the failure to obtain treatment of illnesses as we often refuse to accept the presence of symptoms indicating ill health, thereby delaying a trip to the doctor and the option of early treatment. Similarly, denial plays a significant part in dealing with addiction. Those of us with addiction problems are often in denial that we have a problem.

Sometimes, a person may accept the fact that something negative is happening but deny the seriousness of it. This is called minimization (see below). Also, a person may accept both the fact and the seriousness but deny their responsibility for it. This is called projection (see below).

Denial can prevent us from incorporating unpleasant information about ourselves and have potentially destructive consequences. A friend may tell us our behavior is destructive, but we just dismiss what we are being told by denying that it is correct or denying its relevance. As a mechanism denial can be very powerful, it is not unusual for a person in therapy to stop attending because the therapist is coming too close to a topic the patient wants to keep hidden. They then deny the fact that the therapist was helping them.

Denial is often used as a mechanism to address sexual abuse within a family. It is much 'easier' to deny sexual abuse is taking place than to accept the potential for the family unit to be torn apart. Furthermore, because the perpetrator is a member of the family, other members of the family will be tainted with the negative image associated with the perpetrator.

Examples:

a) Oliver is confronted with evidence that their partner is cheating on them. They deny that the affair is happening and provide excuses to negate any evidence that it is. "She isn't cheating. She was at that hotel for a conference."

b) Emma does not have any close friends, nor does she have a partner. When asked she will say: "I don't need anyone. I am quite happy on my own." People who tell themselves they don't need for friends, intimate relationships or sex are often in denial.

8. **Displacement.** *Concept.* Displacement is when we express feelings to a substitute target (a person or a thing), because we are unwilling to express them to the real target. It is the redirecting of feelings and urges felt about a target but taken out upon another target. We often use displacement when we cannot express our feelings in a safe manner to the person to whom they should be directed. We may punch the wall instead of punching the person who has raised our anger, because we are frightened of that person. Displacement may also involve the shifting of blame for some act, from a person whom we fear onto a less threatening person. This safer target can be a person who is under our control, or someone who is dependent upon us for financial support or well-being.

As a defense mechanism displacement is ineffective and will often lead to other problems. While directing our anger at another party may provide a temporary outlet for our pain, the fact that it is misdirected neither addresses the underlying cause and is very likely to create issues with the person to whom it was misdirected.

When we are uncomfortable with some of our sexual urges, we may displace desires with which we are uncomfortable, into sexual fetishism. This may take the form of being attracted to a specific body part like the feet or an inanimate object such as shoes.

A very destructive form of displacement is when the anger or other negative emotions are redirected towards oneself, instead of to the person to whom they should be directed. This creates self-loathing and is closely linked to depression and suicide.

Examples:

a) Delroy, has grown up with a violent father and wishes he could strike out at him. However, he remains fearful of his father and displaces his desire to strike out to other children in his school class. Bullying is often a sign that the bully has been abused.

b) Teddy knows that his boss was responsible for losing an important client which results in a financial loss for Teddy. Because he is unable to blame the boss, he chooses to displace the blame to an underling, taking his frustration out on them.

c) Colin was raised by emotionally unavailable parents. However, as a child his aunt gave him a sense of affection and love. He spent considerable time with her and often he would massage her feet, to relax her. This was done in return for the kindness she showed him and in a non-sexual way. His aunt provided Teddy with emotional stability and a sense of security. As he grew older, he displaced this emotional security into a sexualized foot fetish.

9. **Dissociation.** *Concept:* When we use dissociation as a defense mechanism, we separate out of our memory things that we don't want to or can't deal with. Dissociation can involve a wide array of experiences from mild detachment from the immediate surroundings to more severe detachment from physical and emotional experiences. The major characteristic of dissociation is a detachment from reality. Dissociation is commonly displayed on a continuum. In mild cases, dissociation can be used to minimize boredom. We all have found ourselves drifting off to think of more pleasant things when listening to a boring lecture or daydreaming when we are on a long journey. Often people will read to escape into a fantasy world leaving behind everyday pressures. In these circumstances we can be said to be disengaged for reality. These activities are, for the most part, harmless.

Further along the continuum, when such activities occur more often or in a more extreme version, they begin to become harmful. If we are constantly daydreaming, we may fail to notice something that could injure us, such as an approaching car. At the farthest end of the continuum the dissociation becomes destructive in its nature. The person may lose all sense of reality and appear robotic during interpersonal exchanges. They may remember a past event, but because of the traumatic nature of that event, dissociate themselves from the feelings they experienced at the time. Reality for a person who dissociates is different from that of other people. They often disconnect from the real world and live in a world of their own creation; one that is uncluttered with feelings or with memories that are unbearable. In extreme cases dissociation can lead to a person believing they have multiple selves.

Dissociation usually originates from a trauma, that has left significant unresolved psychological pain. People who have a history of childhood abuse often suffer from some form of dissociation. Where a child grows up in a dysfunctional, or abusive home the child can become overwhelmed by what is happening around them. In order to cope they dissociate from what is going on around them, in effect, they check out. If this child fails to learn other coping strategies, then they will revert to dissociation when faced with difficulties in later life. This is likely to lead to difficulty in maintaining relationships.

Examples:

a) Maurice grew up in a dysfunctional home where there were often violent arguments between his parents. As a child he often escaped to his room where he created a fantasy world. Now, in later life, when pressure starts to occur in relationships or the work place, he withdraws from the situation and spends a considerable amount of time imagining himself to be somewhere else.

b) Elizabeth was the victim of a violent attack.

While she can describe the event in detail, at no time in the description will she mention the impact the event had on her, or how she feels about it. Her description may well be detailed but it is impersonal.

c) Elaine has had trauma in her early life and during this period relied heavily on dissociation to protect herself. Years later she is very attracted to a man called Henry and keen for the relationship to progress. She 'chooses' to ignore the many warning signs that Henry is not good for her, dissociating the messages that would lead her to ending the relationship. Her previous experiences have conditioned her and now that conditioning is working against her.

10. **Distortion.** *Concept:* Distortion occurs when the person reshapes reality to meet their needs and avoid pain. In using distortion, we deal with things that are causing us stress by altering or reshaping internal or external reality. When we are using distortion, we then tend to act in accordance with the new reality we have created. Our behavior follows our distortion and our position becomes further entrenched when we must justify what we have done.

Selective distortion occurs when we absorb only material which fits our world view. If we hear new information that supports our existing beliefs, we take it in, but we exclude anything that contradicts what we currently believe.

Where we perceive that something that we desire is unattainable, we convince ourselves that it is in some way defective, allowing us to move on. A famous version is Aesop's fable about the fox and the grapes. Unable to reach the grapes the fox tells himself that the grapes are sour. Hence the expression - 'sour grapes.'

Distortion is also one of the more common defense mechanisms used by narcissists. They indulge in the distortion of facts, to enforce their superiority or self-righteousness often to the extent of blatant lying.

Examples:

a) Liam is putting on a lot of weight. He buys large fitting clothes, telling himself that the store in which he is shopping makes clothes that are a closer fitting style.

b) Donald needs to feel popular. At a recent event few people turned up to see him perform. Despite the photographic evidence he claims there was a massive crowd present.

11. **Fantasy.** *Concept:* Fantasy involves creating a world inside our self, when the real world becomes too painful, or difficult, to deal with. Fantasy uses daydreaming and imagination as a method for dealing with anxiety, pain and stress. Fantasy as a defense mechanism can also be about us using wishful thinking. We base decisions and behavior on what we would like our life to be, rather than what the reality is. Fantasy is sometimes about channeling what we think of as unacceptable or unattainable desires into imagination, an obvious example of this being sexual fantasies where we fantasize about some person or some act.

There are positive aspects to using fantasy. If we imagine that we will be successful this may lead to feelings of success, and so act as a rehearsal for our future success. In addition, imagining what fun we will have on a forthcoming holiday is a healthy use of fantasy, especially if we are going through a bad patch at work.

Escaping into a fantasy world can often be aided by things such as computer games, books and television and for many people these are an effective escape from the pressures of life. However, just as fantasy acts as a solution to stress, it may also become part of the problem. When fantasies become the alternative to living, then the behavior is pathological or if our fantasy life exists at the expense of any meaningful encounter with others in the real world, we have a problem. When we deal with emotional stress by retreating into excessive daydreaming as a substitute for human relationships, it is likely to result in difficulties for us developing the skills to deal with the problems of everyday life. Also, imagining solutions to problems, instead of really solving them has negative consequences.

A repeated retreat into a fantasy world can become serious and self-perpetuating. Once a person begins to gain comfort from living the type of life where they relish solitude and where they fantasize about not having to bother about other people, they develop greater self-containment and self-reliance. Their world becomes one where they think they do not need any one to satisfy the fundamental human need of belonging. In turn, this enhances their ability to live alone without feeling isolated. Interpersonal intimacy is avoided, and their often-eccentric ways serve to keep others at a distance. They fall further into a fantasy life but one which they cannot see.

The fantasy defense mechanism is similar in many aspects to dissociation.

Examples:

a) Roger tells himself his promotion interview went 'really well' and begins to imagine himself in the new job. The reality is that he answered many of the questions badly.

b) Tim spends the greater part of his time playing fantasy-based computer games where he takes on the role of the hero. He does this to the exclusion of all other social contact. In time he never leaves his bedroom but believes himself to be one of the characters in a game.

c) Elizabeth spends all her free time she has reading romance novels, as she can escape the problems in her life. The amount of time she spends doing this means she avoids normal social interaction, but in her mind, she 'is just an avid reader.' She has hundreds of books but few friends.

12. **Humor** *Concept:* Humor, when used as a defense mechanism, is the is making of a joke out of a painful situation. It can involve changing uncomfortable feelings into a humorous act or story. When we look for the funny aspect in a situation in which we are frightened or lack control, it can help us endure it. Humor can reduce the intensity of a situation and can help us by giving as a different perspective on it. Humor can also help other people deal with a serious situation. If they see us being able to smile about the event it can boost their mood sufficiently to help

them cope.

Many people will be familiar with the concept of 'dark' or 'black' humor where jokes are made about very serious or sad subjects. This type of humor is very prevalent in policing, or other emergency services, who face serious or upsetting events on a very regular basis. Sometimes referred to as 'canteen' humor, (the police canteen being the place where one could once hear such jokes) this mechanism was an effective strategy to deal with the mental stress brought about by the day-to-day events of policing. While to the ears of outsiders the topics covered were inappropriate or dark, it allowed release for those involved in bad events.

There can be real benefits to using humor and it is looked upon as a 'mature' defense mechanism. However, there can be a downside to its use. Sometimes we over use it. We use it in situations where it is not appropriate, to mask our own discomfort about what is happening. We laugh to cover our embarrassment, and to hide the reality of how much we are hurting. We may also use humor to avoid conflict but the problem with this is that the conflict still exists and continues to eat away at us.

Examples:

a) Angela dislikes any form of conflict. When she is annoyed at someone or something, she may pass a comment, but she will always giggle at the end of the sentence. Subconsciously the message she is conveying is: "Please don't take anything I have just said seriously." The giggle is intended to make the listener less likely to continue the conflict.

b) Gregory is embarrassed about any discussion of a sexual nature. Every time something of a sexual nature comes up in a conversation his comments are always accompanied by a forced laughter.

13. **Idealization**. *Concept:* Idealization occurs when a person attributes exaggerated positive qualities to another person. It is where we can see only good or bad in a person. Idealization is a form of splitting (see below). In child development, idealization of a parent is normal but if development is interrupted by trauma, use of this defense mechanism may persist into adulthood.

If we are in a depressed state, we are more likely to idealize someone, as we see them as a potential escape route from our current feelings. We will attribute exclusively positive qualities to them and initially, we may have a profound sense of infatuation with them. This feeling can alleviate any sense of sadness or despair we are feeling at the time. However, as reality sinks in that infatuation will wear off and after a period we will return to our state of depression. It is likely that our pain/sadness will have increased because our idealized person has failed to live up to our (unrealistic) expectations. What is frustrating about this position is that it is often our actions that have led to the person withdrawing from us. Our expectations of them and our needy behavior will likely have been suffocating for them. The fact that we were unable to see this at the time, is a strong indicator of how our existing state has distorted our thinking and how ineffective this defense mechanism has been.

Example:

a) Joel has had a troubled upbringing. He becomes involved in a religious cult and he idolizes the cult leader. He is 'blind' to the leader's many faults and his physical and sexual abuse of other cult members.

14. **Identification.** *Concept*: See Introjection

15. **Intellectualization.** *Concept:* Intellectualization occurs where the person avoids uncomfortable emotions by focusing on facts and logic. The situation that causes them pain is treated as an interesting problem that the person can discuss on an intellectual basis. The emotional aspects are completely ignored. The person thinks more to feel less. Intellectualization allows a person to analyze an event in a way that does not cause them anxiety. In short, it involves removing the emotion from emotional experiences, and leads to discussing painful events in detached and seemingly uncaring, ways. Prolonged use of this defense mechanism may lead the person to become distant from their feelings. When asked to describe those feelings they may find it difficult to use emotional language or to accurately describe what they feel.

Examples:

a) Elaine has been brought up by a very dominant and controlling father and has feelings of anger and hurt towards him. Instead of facing those feelings and the trauma his actions have caused her she chooses to describe her father using language that avoids any expression of her feelings. "My father was quite strict." "He always liked to have his way." In discussing him, she omits how he made her feel focusing only on actualities.

b) Matthew on being diagnosed with a terminal illness may spend significant time researching on the internet, learning everything about the illness, instead of reacting emotionally to the diagnosis. He chooses to discuss the pros and cons of various treatments. Thus, allowing him to block out the feelings.

16. **Introjection.** Concept: Introjection occurs when a person unconsciously takes on the ideas and beliefs of another person or group, in order to conform to the expectations of that person or group, thus avoiding the potential pain that stems from non-conformation. Introjection is about accepting another person's attitudes and values as our own. These external values will have been communicated to us overtly and covertly, and through verbal and non-verbal communication, by someone we admire or rely upon.

Introjection can take place in quite simple forms. For example: A group of young people all choose to dress in a similar manner and to speak using the same street slang. In these circumstances the group may be emulating the behavior and attitudes of a dominant person in their group.

Introjection often occurs in childhood were the

child, seeking acceptance by the parents, takes on the behaviors and language of the parent. We may also introject the standards of our culture or religion in order to be accepted by them and so preserve a positive self-image. We take in so much of our parents in our formative years, at an unconscious level, that we are surprised in later life when we turn out to be like them in so many ways despite our denials that this is the case.

Identification occurs when a person not only takes on a beliefs of another person group or cause, but also begins to identify with that person group or cause. Identification is about identifying with some idea or object so deeply, that it becomes a part of us.

The concept of identification is very similar to that of introjection and it can be useful to regard the two as being at either end of a continuum. The line where one crosses to the other is not fixed. As can be seen in Figure 3.1, a person starts with introjection of another's values, they then internalize these values, and move to a place where they can be said to have identified with that person.

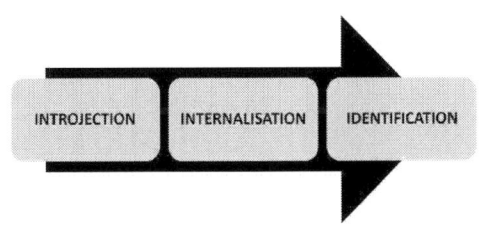

Figure 3.1 Introjection to Identification

In the identification stage we modify our image, values and behavior patterns in order to be like the object with which we have identified. This identification usually involves the emulation of the person's skills or abilities, the taking on of their characteristics and a feeling of self-esteem to be affiliated with them.

Identification is often seen in the behavior of sports fans who follow a particular team. They always want to wear the latest team shirt and have other paraphernalia associated with the team. This fact is not lost on the sports teams who exploit this identification for financial gain.

Identification with an aggressor occurs when some-one is abused and begins to act like the aggressor by abusing others. Use of identification in this way is often associated with antisocial personality disorder. The person goes on to harm others because unconsciously, they want others to feel the same pain they felt.

Examples:

a) Louise and Robert are a married couple but have ongoing marital issues. Louise resents the fact Robert holds the views that looking after the home is a wife's role. Robert says that his father always expected his mother to do the housework and he believes the same. At this point Robert is introjecting the values of his father. He merely believes.

b) If Robert had internalized the views of his father and then expected Louise to undertake a similar role as his mother, then it would be said that identification had taken place. Robert has identi-fied with his father's belief's and has adopted an identical role as his father. As a result of this identification Robert now expects Louise to treat him, as his mother treated his father. Belief is accompanied by action.

c) Chester always had a dislike of guns but because his best friend is a keen hunter Chester takes that up as an avid interest.

d) Martha has for a long time been obsessed with a movie star. She has styled her hair in the same way and dressed in similar clothing. She knows the words to all her movies. The movie star committed suicide at a young age and Martha does the same on reaching that age.

17. **Isolation** *Concept:* Isolation involves creating a mental barrier between some threatening thought and other, everyday thoughts and feelings. The person takes a problem or conflict and shuts it off in a corner of the mind, isolating it from normal day to day thought processes. By doing so the person is saying: "I will not allow this bad thought to come into contact with other thoughts or to form connections with them." Without associated connections, the perceived threat will not be remembered as often and is less likely to impact on other aspects of mental activity. As a defense mechanism isolation does not actually remove the threatening idea from mental existence, it just minimizes its impact for the person. In doing so this reduces any effect on the person's self-esteem.

Another relevant form of isolation is known as temporal bracketing. In essence, we isolate previous misdeeds or failures by 'burying' them in the past, creating the idea of an 'old' me which I don't like, and a 'new' me which I do.

If we use isolation as a defense mechanism, we may give no external clue to the conflict we are experiencing, except for a tendency not to react when a reaction would be the norm.

Example:

a) Alexander has led a life which he now finds difficult to face. He drank heavily, neglected family duties and had numerous adulterous relationships. He undergoes a religious conversion and proclaims himself to be 'born again'. Anything that occurred before his conversion is now experienced separately from his previous history.

18. **Justification.** *Concept:* Justification is typically used in a situation where a moral standpoint is being taken and the person is seeking to explain why they have taken that standpoint: 'I am justified in believing this because…' or 'I am justified in not doing this because….' Justification comes into play when the topic is about right or wrong. Because moral issues are part of everyday life, we can see it playing out daily. Often those in the public eye, such as politicians, will seek to justify their actions when they have been criticized for some moral lapse.

One of the common challenges in today's world is the so called 'entitlement mentality.' People expect to have the things they want. If someone does not have what they want, they feel justified in taking it. If confronted with what they have done, they say that what they did was right because they had no other way of getting it. The behavior then becomes justified in their eyes. In a similar way, terrorists justify their acts of barbarity.

Examples:

a) Jacob has had an affair. He justifies his actions by stating that his wife had been ignoring him at home and he needed feelings of intimacy.

b) Bert steals from his employer. He justifies his actions by claiming his employer was not paying him for overtime he worked.

19. **Minimization.** *Concept:* Minimization occurs when we deny how serious something is or when we admit the fact but deny its seriousness. When we minimize, we technically accept what has occurred but only in a watered-down form. Minimization involves aspects of denial and rationalization in situations where complete denial won't be believed. Minimization is a common strategy in dealing with feelings of guilt.

In using minimizations. we are attempting to convince someone else that the bad thing we did wasn't really as bad as we both know it was. When we use this as a defense, we are very likely to repeat the behavior as we do not accept the importance in correcting it. Students will often use minimization in relation to assessed exercises: 'I didn't do it that badly.' or 'It wasn't as bad as it looked.' or 'I knew the theory; I just got a bit muddled in applying it.'

Minimization may also involve:

a) Avoiding acknowledging and dealing with negative emotions by reducing the importance and impact of events that give rise to those emotions.

b) Avoiding the conscious confrontation with the negative impacts of our behavior on others, by reducing the perception of such impacts.

c) Avoiding interpersonal confrontation, by reducing the perception of the impact of someone else's behavior on us.

Minimization is sometimes thought of as a cognitive distortion as opposed to a defense mechanism. (Cognitive distortions are more fully explained in the chapter 4.)

Examples:

a) Charlotte smokes and is aware of the related health problems. She describes herself as a "social smoker." This allows her to convince herself she is not smoking all the time and therefore, her health is at less risk.

b) Todd has been caught having an affair. When confronted by his wife he states: "It was just sex; it didn't mean anything."

20. **Passive Aggression.** Concept: Passive aggression involves dealing with stress by indirectly and unassertively expressing aggression toward others. It is characterized by indirect resistance to the demands of others and an avoidance of direct confrontation (Kantor, 2002). With passive aggression there is a person at whom we want to strike out (the target),

but because this target holds a position of power compared to us, or they are physically stronger than us, we adopt a strategy of striking out at them in a way that is not obvious to them. Outwardly, we may display cooperation but this outward display hides are true feelings and intentions.

Our actions are likely to include resentment and resistance. Instead of coming out and saying how we feel, we make snide remarks or make digs at the target but mask them in humor. If there is something the target wants us to do, we don't tell them we won't do what they have asked, but we will procrastinate. We may do it badly or 'forget' to do it and we will certainly do it with sullenness, making cheap jibes as we go.

With passive aggressive behavior the person doing it will often be unaware of exactly what they are doing. This is because:

a) They are hurting because of what the other person has done.

b) They want to respond to alleviate that pain.

c) They are frightened to respond.

d) They don't want to admit they are frightened because this damages their self-image and thereby, cause themselves more pain.

Passive aggression is often used by children towards parents or teachers. A failure to develop effective communication skills means that they continue to rely on this defense into adulthood. Passive aggressive behavior by the victim is also common in abusive relationships because the abuser would punish any attempt made at direct or assertive communication.

If we are on the receiving side of passive aggressive behavior it is extremely difficult to counteract. By its very nature it is clandestine and the person using it creates a position where they can deny any wrong doing. What we need to remember is that passive aggression is a defense mechanism rather than an attack method, so if it is occurring, we need to look to see what is causing the person to feel threatened or upset.

Examples

a) Raj feels demeaned by the task his boss has set him at work. He is upset because he feels he was overlooked for a different task that he wanted to do. He is frightened of saying to his boss, but he cannot refuse to do the new task. He adopts a passive aggressive approach, seeking clarification on innocuous points, and engages in other time-wasting tactics. Any work he submits is always submitted at the last minute.

b) Mary has had an argument with her husband and in order to punish him she 'forgets' to mention to him that his mother telephoned earlier and wanted him to call back.

21. **Projection.** *Concept:* Projection is the shifting our own unacceptable thoughts, feelings or actions onto someone else to avoid feelings of guilt, shame or regret. Projection is used especially when the thoughts we are having are considered to unacceptable for us to express, or we may feel completely ill at ease with

having those thoughts. Projection is often the result of a lack of insight into our own motives and feelings and/or a lack of acknowledgement of those motives. It may involve perceiving others as having traits that we inaccurately believe we do not have. Projection reflects our tendency to reject what we don't like about ourselves. The pot calling the kettle black, exemplifies the idea of projection.

With projection, the fault lies with us, but is shifted by us to avoid blame. With displacement (See above), the fault lies outside of us, but is still shifted by us, to displace blame to another person.

Examples:

a) Anthony has been thinking about cheating on his wife. To cover up his feelings of guilt about such thoughts he begins to imagine she is having an affair and accuses her of it.

b) Amber never listens to what her partner is saying. She frequently gets angry and blames her partner for not listening. The reality is that it is Amber who is at fault, but she does not want to accept that.

c) Belinda has prejudices against people of different races. She does not want to recognize this trait in herself and projects those feelings onto others on her campus, accusing the dean of racially based discrimination.

Variation: **Projective identification.** Concept: projective identification is like projection but in this case the person on whom we have projected the negative thoughts, eventually identifies with those negative thoughts and internalizes them. Projective identification often occurs in a dysfunctional relationship where one party uses it as a device to control the other. For example: An abusive wife will use it to control her partner, getting them to accept the blame for the dysfunction in the relationship. The way it is used is like projection but has one extra step:

Example (part 1):

a) Yvette has a large cold sore on her lip about which she feels very self-conscious and insecure.

b) As Yvette walks into work, her colleague Jackson looks up and says 'Hello'. Yvette imagines he is staring at the cold sore.

c) Yvette lashes out at Jackson saying: "Alright, I have a cold sore but stop staring at it." Yvette is projecting her insecurities onto Jackson.

This is a case of projection. Yvette has projected her uncomfortable feelings onto Jackson

Example (part 2):

a) Yvette has a large cold sore on her lip about which she feels very self-conscious.

b) As Yvette walks into work, her colleague Jackson looks up and says 'Hello'. Yvette imagines he is staring at the cold sore.

c) Yvette lashes out at Jackson saying: "Alright, I have a cold sore but stop staring at it." Yvette is projecting her insecurities onto Jackson.

d) Jackson takes on board Yvette's comments and begins to think he was staring, and this makes him feel very uncomfortable. Jackson has identified with the comment.

This is a case of projective identification. Yvette has projected her uncomfortable feelings onto Jackson, and he has accepted them. In the scenario Yvette is using the mechanism to control Jackson's behavior.

22. **Rationalization.** *Concept:* Rationalization occurs when a person deals with emotional conflict or stress by concealing the true motivations for their thoughts, actions, or feelings through the construction of reassuring or self-serving but false accounts for their actions. It is about making excuses. It occurs when we try to explain away behavior which conflicts with our feelings or values, and we make up 'logical' reasons to explain why we have done something, making it seem entirely rational, when in fact we were driven by motives we don't want to acknowledge, not even to ourselves.

We may rationalize violating our long-term goals in order to gratify our immediate desires; that is, we lie to ourselves in order to get what we want right now rather than waiting for long-term gratification. Then we repeat our rationalizations or create more in order to shore up our defense.

Rationalization is a particularly common mechanism for those with sensitive egos. If we hear ourselves explaining, again and again, why we shouldn't feel ashamed or guilty, about something we have done then, chances are, part of us knows we should not have done it.

Examples:

a) Brendan smacks his child and says it is for the child's own good. He explains that his father did the same with him and he suffered no harm because of it.

b) Rees buys an expensive car and then tells everyone his old car was unreliable or unsafe.

c) Toby is on a diet but eats a large chocolate bar. He tells himself he deserves it because he has had a hard day at work, and he will go straight back on the diet in the morning.

23. **Reaction Formation.** *Concept:* Reaction formation involves converting a socially unacceptable impulse into its opposite. It occurs when we act in way that is directly opposite to what we are actually feeling. With reaction formation, we go beyond denial - we act in a way that is opposite to which we think or feel. Typically, reaction formation is marked by a blatant act that is contrary to our beliefs.

It may be that we have a trait that is socially unacceptable, so we change our behavior in a way that shows others that we have the opposite trait. We may hide our racist feelings with overt expressions that are anti-racist.

Perhaps the most widely quoted reference to reaction formation is that of Shakespeare's "The lady doth protest too much, methinks" (Hamlet, III, ii). In this scene the inference is that the lady in question protests about the allegation of murder are so over-the-top to be credible.

Narcissists often use reaction formation as a defense mechanism. They present us with an idealized, false outward impression of themselves, in the desire for our admiration. This is done to prevent us from seeing how damaged and insecure they are on the inside. Their unconscious fear of being exposed, translates into a desire to be watched and this in turn results in attention seeking behavior.

Serious forms of reaction formation result in profound unconscious anger, anger that is often turned inward, resulting in lifetime battles with depression.

Examples:

a) Ricky gave up cigarettes several months previously and is now repulsed by the smell of cigarettes. He has become very vocal about his support for anti-smoking legislation.

b) Brice is sexually attracted to men. However, he feels his homosexuality would not be accepted by his friends or family. In order to mask his true feelings, especially from himself, he is often outspoken in his condemnation of same sex relationships. In more extreme cases this may escalate into carrying out violent attacks on young men emerging from gay bars.

c) Christopher is a shy person and finds sexual desire to be frightening. In order to cope with his fears and to keep his own sexual impulses at bay, adopts a very puritanical and disapproving attitude about the sexual behavior of others. As this attitude increases Christopher may become develop feelings of repulsion about his own sexual organs.

24. **Regression.** *Concept:* Regression is an attempt to ease pain or discomfort by reverting to behaviors that worked for us in our earlier life. We use methods that worked in our childhood as a way of protecting ourselves from having to confront the present-day reality. Our behavior becomes more childish and instead of using mature problem-solving behavior to deal with a situation, we resort to actions such as stomping our feet, slamming doors or sulking. We often resort to such behavior because it is our port of first call when under stress and it is intellectually less demanding. The problem with this type of behavior is that such behavior is destructive in nature and we often later regret it. Not only that, but it often means there are more fences to mend than there were when we first resorted to the behavior. Some people have compared regression to stepping into a time machine which whisks us back to a time when we last felt safe and where things were not so psychologically complicated.

Another aspect of regression is that with it we can mentally return to an earlier time in our life when we were not so threatened with negative self-concepts. We go back to a time when we had no negative self-image and we can then see ourselves now, as we did back then. Our behavior follows our mind and we behave in a way that draws comments such as: 'You are behaving like a spoiled brat.' or we might be referred to as being '...a proper little princess.'

Examples:

a) Ella, a young woman, might curl up into the fetal position after a relationship breakup and refuse to get out of bed[4].

b) Paul, a teenager, who is being bullied at school might begin bed-wetting a habit he had left behind as a young child. This is a strong indicator for any parent that something unsavory is happening in the child's life and something they do not want to discuss.

c) Frank wants to watch sport on television, but his wife Marcia wants to go to the shopping center. Rather than resolving the issue through discussion Frank agrees to go but spends the afternoon taking no interest in anything going on and replying to Marcia's attempts at conversation with one-word answers.

25. **Repression.** *Concept:* Repression is the unconscious and seemingly involuntary removal from awareness of the negative self-concepts that our ego finds too painful to tolerate. It is the unconscious blocking of unacceptable thoughts, feelings and painful events. There are two parts to it. First, it is an unconscious action; we aren't aware, we have done it. Second, it is an involuntary action; our ego simply removes it from conscious awareness without asking. The key to repression is that people do it unconsciously, so

---

[4] Actually, so might a middle-aged man. At least that's what a friend told me.

they often have very little control over it. With repression, our mind makes the decision to bury a memory in the unconscious, thereby ensuring painful, disturbing or dangerous thoughts are kept hidden. A common example of repression occurs with child abuse or other traumatic experiences that occurred early on in our development. When such events occur, a child does not have the mental capacity to deal with them and the most effective thing to do is to bury them. While repression, much like denial, may serve to remove the immediate pain of an experience, if we do not eventually process and deal with the experience it can have severe consequences later. Repressed memories have the habit of dictating our behavior in later life, with us having no conscious awareness of why we are behaving in that way. Often victims of trauma will develop the need for obsessive levels of control, indicated by things such as extreme tidiness or obsessive washing. Lack of flexibility in moral judgements can be another indicator of repressed memories. Here, the person adopts rigid moral stances that appear to others to be excessive or inappropriate for the given circumstances.

Just because we are not consciously aware of how much anger we feel toward our father, that doesn't mean the anger has disappeared. It will inevitably continue to make its presence known in covert ways – humorous little digs, for instance, or sarcasm. If we feel little or no interest in sex, we almost certainly have repressed our desire. There is a fine line between denial and repression. But where denial involves the outright refusal to accept a given reality, repression involves completely forgetting the experience altogether. While repression, much like denial, may serve immediate purposes, particularly if we were tormented by a painful experience, if we do not eventually process and deal with the experience it can have severe consequences later.

Example:

a) Baxter was sexually abused as a child. He has blocked all conscious awareness of the incidents but showers 3 or 4 times a day because 'he never feels clean'.

26. **Somatization.** Concept: Somatization is the manifestation of psychological distress by the presentation of somatic symptoms (symptoms of the body). Somatization involves experiencing physical symptoms in lieu of emotional ones. With somatization, when we are undergoing stress or emotional difficulties, we divert the psychological pain into physical symptoms that suggest we are physically unwell. Because we are unaware, we have translated the psychological pain into physical pain, we seek medical help. However, because there is no underlying physical condition, a doctor cannot explain the symptoms. This is obviously problematic for a doctor. A person suffering in this way is not 'faking' illness, but the origin of the problem is mental, not physical. Neither they nor the doctor realize this.

Most people experience somatization at some point in their lives. Many of us will have felt the desire to 'throw up' before some forthcoming event as it is making us nervous, and most of us will have suffered at one time or another from a headache brought on by stress. These are examples of somatization at work. However, people who regularly find this occurring, over a prolonged period may be diagnosed as suffering from a somatoform disorder.

Somatization can be effective under certain circumstances. When the unconscious mind is suffering from psychological pain which is not being addressed, it gets attention by attacking the physical body. The person then starts to pay attention to the physical ailment, which then forces them to slow down and potentially provides the space to alleviate the psychological issue.

Somatization is sometimes referred to as 'conversion' A person anxious about completing or unable to complete a task for their manger may convert the anxiety into some 'illness' that provides them with a face-saving excuse for not completing the task.

The connection between mental well-being and physical well-being is widely accepted. Most readers will be familiar with the use of placebos to cause a person to recover from illness. Somatization is the reverse effect.

Examples:

a) This defense is familiar to all of us. As children we learned to tell our parents: 'My belly is sore. I can't go to school.' This could be used as a mask to avoid school rather than stating the reality that we were fearful of something at school. There was no way for a parent to prove if we were sick or not. While it is normal for stresses and strains in a child's life to be expressed in bodily pains (sometimes referred to as growing pains) there is evidence to suggest that where particular attention is paid to these complaints, children are significantly more likely to use somatization as a defense in later life.

b) Raphael is a police officer working in a high-pressure environment where there is significant danger involved. Added to this is stress stemming from management issues. He begins to suffer from chronic headaches and muscular pains for which the doctor can find no physical problem.

c) Taylor, a student, has told all his colleagues he will be successful on a course that requires extensive physical effort. As the course progresses Taylor realizes, he will not be successful and so he develops a sore back. 'Ah, but for my injury I would have completed the course.' Much better for Taylor to protect both his public image and his self-images than the reality: 'I wasn't fit enough.' This mechanism can be so powerful that Taylor genuinely believes he has a sore back.

27. **Splitting.** *Concept*: Splitting is a mechanism that allows a person to control their unease about a situation by dividing their perception of it into two separate and opposing sides. When splitting occurs, the person will perceive the situation in terms of black or white. When viewing another person, they will see that person in terms of all good or all bad.

As people, we do not like things that are ambiguous or confusing. Being in this state is a difficult place for many to be in. A way we can manage this is to split the reality into two separate camps: either/or. This provides us with a sense of certainty and leaves us believing we have a clear understanding about what we are encountering and how we should behave towards it. We don't.

Splitting is normal during childhood, where we perceive things in an oversimplified way. The fairy stories we are told are full of heroes and monsters and are constructed as good versus bad. However, early trauma in life can lead us to continuing to rely on splitting as a defense mechanism to get us through adult life. This prevents us from taking a more realistic view of life. We fail to see the complexity in situations or in others. While spitting may make us feel less anguished it is detrimental to relationships. Our inability to grasp the nuances of a relationship, to accept having mixed emotions or to accept that we are all, a blend of good and bad traits, means we find it difficult to maintain relationships. We are likely to resort to all or nothing feelings for a person and move rapidly from strong positive feelings to strong negative feelings.

Splitting also helps us to reinforce positive feelings about ourselves, as we can demonize others. Splitting can also have a significant impact on a group leading to those in the group perceiving themselves as all good and those outside the group as all bad. We will often see splitting where there is racism or xenophobia.

A more extreme version of splitting is fragmentation. Where splitting is about two opposing views fragmentation is about many different views that cannot be reconciled.

Examples:

a) Issac is deeply religious. He sees the world in terms solely of good and evil. You either follow his faith in the way he demands, in which case you are eternally blessed, or you don't, and you are eternally damned. There is no room for anything in between.

b) Irwin's parents have recently become divorced and he is struggling with the break up. He does not have the mental capacity to deal with seeing the complexity of the issue at hand. In order to cope with the situation, he chooses to side with his mother, idolizing her and spurning his father. His mother can do no wrong and his father no right.

28. **Sublimation.** *Concept:* Sublimation is simply the channeling of unacceptable impulses, and emotions into more acceptable ones. Sublimation involves taking a desire that is perceived as being fundamentally antisocial or unacceptable and channeling the energy into socially valued activities.

Sigmund Freud's most common allusion to sublimation related to how sexual instincts could be channeled into artistic or intellectual actions. However, in considering this one must remember the prevailing views of sexual activities at the time of Freud's work, and the fact that many sexual feelings that would now be perceived as normal, would then have been perceived as abnormal.

Sublimation is closely related to 'displacement', as it involves the redirection of impulses. Nevertheless, sublimation is considered the healthier of the options, because it can involves refocusing harmful impulses into productive ones. Using sublimation can help a person transfer energy to a healthy pursuit that otherwise would be lost or used in a manner that might cause the person more anxiety.

Examples:

a) Agnes lost her son to a terminal illness. She has started a charity to find a cure for the disease. Engaging in charitable activities enables her to cope with the pain the loss of a loved one has brought about.

b) Joseph has sexual impulses that conflict with his strong religious beliefs. So that he can remove the anxiety these feelings cause him, Joseph obsessively takes part in rigorous exercise.

c) In a more constructive act of sublimation, Anthony, who is aware he has anger issues, enrolls in a kickboxing class to channel the anger and aggression in a more constructive way.

29. **Suppression.** *Concept:* Suppression is the conscious removal from our mind of negative self-concepts that we find intolerable. It involves consciously attempting to stop thinking about a particular thought. The irony is that often when we try to suppress thoughts the frequency of those thoughts increases, and it seems we can think about little else. For this reason, trying to suppress an upsetting thought may be an ineffective strategy. Suppression is sometimes confused with repression, but they are not the same. Suppression is a conscious effort.

Because suppression is often regarded as a deliberate choice it could therefore be thought of more as a coping strategy than a defense mechanism. With the use of suppression as a coping strategy we choose to make a conscious decision to delay paying attention to a thought or an emotion, so that we can cope with whatever else is going on in our life, at the relevant time but we are not attempting to hide the negative thing away. We are acknowledging the presence of the uncomfortable or distressing emotions while accepting that we will have to return to them at a later stage. It really depends on the amount of conscious thought we put into the action as to whether it is a defense mechanism or coping strategy and what we are hoping to achieve. It is important that we recognize which way we are using suppression.

Examples:

a) Anya gets upset with the behavior of her brother. She decides that she will not think about what he has been doing.

b) Alex has been deeply offended by comments his boss has made about the professionalism of his work. As he has a lot going on at present, he decides to avoid discussing the matter until the following week. "I will put it off to then, so I can deal with it properly. I am just too busy at the minute."

30. **Undoing.** *Concept:* Undoing is based on the idea that it is possible to make amends, or to correct mistakes by doing some new action, which is the opposite of the original bad action. This rests in the hope that the new action will balance out the wrong done in the

previous action. If we have said or done something and that has created in us unpleasant feelings, such as guilt, we will want to alleviate these feelings and avoid the discomfort. We now want to make up for the bad thing by doing a good thing. It is not necessary for the person to be aware we have done something bad or even for us to have done something, for negative feelings to arise, and for us to resort to using this defense. It may merely be that one person had prejudiced thoughts about another and now wants to make up for having those thoughts.

Undoing forms a part of many religions and is found in the concept of penance; the seeking of forgiveness often by carrying our ritualistic acts. These can include such things as reciting prayers numerous times and completing a symbolic gesture. ("Say three Hail Mary's and light a candle."). More extreme rituals may dictate such things as self-flagellation or similar acts of self-harm. As these ritualistic acts don't do anything to undo the harm, they are as much an act of symbolism as anything. Ironically, they can make the person feel better, which for them, is what the undoing is really about.

A less extreme form of undoing takes the form of rumination over past events. We have done something we regret, and we replay the event repeatedly in our head, thinking how we could have done things differently, often coming up with fanciful ways it would then have played out.

Translation of Freud's original German word 'Ungeschehenmachen' provides a clearer understanding of the problem with this defense mechanism. The word translates as "un-make happen". As it is impossible to make something that has happened, 'unhappen', the use of the mechanism of undoing is pathological. We can't undo the past.

Examples:

a) After ridiculing Marta's (a student) answer in class, Greg, the teacher, might try to undo his actions by spending the next hour praising the Marta's positive qualities. This is likely to make no difference as she will still remember the slight.

b) Donald, a millionaire, gives to charities supporting poverty to make up for guilt he feels from exploiting the poor to make his money. In the Bible we can read one such story where Jesus has confronted a tax collector: "But Zacchaeus stood up and said to the Lord, "Look, Lord! Here and now I give half of my possessions to the poor, and if I have cheated anybody out of anything, I will pay back four times the amount." (Luke 19:8 Bible New English Version)

c) Another biblical related example is that of Pontius Pilates 'washing of hands' where he distances himself from any harm set to befall Jesus. By washing his hands, he attempts to cleanse himself from an act he feels bad about. Obsessive washing is also common with the victims of sexual abuse who do it in attempt to feel clean and undo the 'dirty' feeling they have because of the abuse.

d) Another all too common example for parents is that of buying our children gifts because we feel guilty about not spending enough time with them. The gifts are intended to make amends for not being there.[5]

31. **Withdrawal.** *Concept:* Withdrawal refers to the tendency to avoid situations that we may experience which are for us, emotionally or psychologically challenging. Withdrawal is about taking us away from anything that carries reminders of painful or stressful thoughts, and emotions. If we think something is going to cause us pain, we avoid it. This may sound well in theory, if there is only one thing that we want to avoid. However, life involves many situations and any of these can be connected to the painful event. It is very difficult to withdraw from one thing without having to withdraw from many others. The withdrawal is likely to escalate. One of our friends may remind us of the event so we withdraw from them. Other friends may notice this behavior and ask uncomfortable questions, so we withdraw from them. Eventually, we lose our social life. Furthermore, we may begin to avoid watching television because there are painful reminders there. Eventually the withdrawal becomes all-consuming and we are all but paralyzed in our own life. Withdrawal can lead to feelings of alienation and loneliness, which create more anxiety and pain.

Although a common tactic for children to use (huffing, sulking, etc.) serious long-term withdrawal carries with it significant dangers, if it persists throughout childhood and into adolescence. Socially withdrawn children

---

[5] "Dad didn't even buy us presents to make up for his neglect." (My daughter wrote that bit.)

are at much greater risk for negative adjustment out-comes, including anxiety, low self-esteem, depressive symptoms, and internalizing problems. They are likely to have difficulties with their peers including rejection, and poor friendship quality and they are likely to have diffi-culties in school in relation to poor relationships with teachers and absenteeism. (Rubin et al., 2009)

Example:

a) As a child Anne was embarrassed because she wet herself at a friend's birthday party. She re-mains frightened of being in a group of people in a strange place. Her friends want her to go with them to social events, but she doesn't feel com-fortable, so she withdraws from her friends. The problem escalates to where she is afraid to go out, eventually becoming more and more reclu-sive in her house.

3.3 Conclusion

As can be seen there is significant cross-over with many of the defense mechanisms. It is difficult to specify exactly what characteristics are specifically associated with which defense mechanism. This reflects the way we use them in life. We rarely stick to one specific mecha-nism, choosing instead to adopt a shotgun like approach, throwing several defenses out there, in the oft vain hope that one of them will ease our pain. However, by listen-ing to exactly what a person is saying and attempting to identify and label which mechanisms are being used and which ones dominate, we have a much better chance of getting to the root of a person's problem and dealing with it.

Now that we know the specifics of each defense mechanism we can move forward and put some context around where they sit in everyday life and their level of effectiveness.

4 - Defense Mechanisms In Context

"The worse deceit is self-deceit."

David Ben-Gurion (1986 -1973)

"Most men would rather deny a hard truth than face it."

A Game of Thrones - George R.R. Martin

4.1 Introduction

N ow that we have a better understanding of each defense mechanism, in this chapter we will examine how they play out in the context of everyday life. We will look at how we can use defense mechanisms in a constructive way and how we can avoid some of the pitfalls associated with them. We will also take a brief look at some other aspects of psychology that will put some context around defense mechanisms.

4.2 Levels of defense mechanism

George Vaillant (1992) put forward the idea that defense mechanisms could be viewed in a hierarchical way. In Vaillant's categorization, he provides a continuum of four levels moving from more primitive to more developed:

Level 1: Pathological defenses. These permit one to effectively rearrange external experiences and eliminate the need to cope with reality.

Level 2: Immature defenses. These lessen distress and anxiety provoked by threatening people or by an uncomfortable reality.

Level 3: Neurotic defenses. Such defenses have short-term advantages in easing pain, but can often cause long-term problems in relationships, work and in enjoying life, especially when used as one's primary style of coping with the world.

Level 4: Mature defenses. These enhance pleasure and feelings of control, helping us to integrate conflicting emotions and thoughts, while we remain productive.

When we develop, we become more mature; we develop more sophisticated means of dealing with problems and in the process, we discard less sophisticated and less effective means. However, sometimes because of circumstances or events in our life, we get stuck and fail to move past developmental markers. We fail to progress to a stage where we have more effective ways of dealing with problems. We may have aged chronologically and may function effectively in most aspects of our life but under specific or stressful circumstances we revert to child-like or primitive behavior. The more primitive or lower level a defense mechanism is, the less likely it is to work for us. We will now explore these levels in more detail and as we work through them it is possible to use our life experience to identify examples of when we have seen the various mechanisms at play and their correlation to our development from childhood to adulthood.

4.3 Pathological defenses

The most primitive defense mechanisms are childlike in form. They are often based on a mistaken or inaccurate representation of social reality. In essence, they allow us to eliminate reality. Though they may work as a means of avoiding short term pain, they do not result in constructive outcomes and are an ineffective means to solve the actual problem. People who use pathological defenses often come across as behaving in an irrational way and because their behavior does not appear in anyway logical, it can be very difficult for another person to grasp or deal with. Conflict can arise rapidly. Most of us have met an adult who functions under certain circumstances in pathological way.

If we have been harmed in some significant way during childhood, we are far more likely to resort to pathological defenses when under stress. These defense mechanisms will have become ingrained to protect us, when we had no other mechanism to do so. The requirement to first confront the childhood event that has caused the trauma, before dealing with the reliance on these mechanisms, means they can be very difficult to overcome and eliminate from the person's behavior.

Pathological defenses include:

a) Conversion.

b) Denial.

c) Splitting.

d) Distortion.

4.4 Immature defenses

Immature defenses are present in adults but more commonly found in adolescents. They are associated with difficulty regulating, expressing, and understanding emotional experiences. Immature defense mechanisms will often be encountered in an environment where normally emotionally stable individuals are confronted by a person they find threatening, or by a set of circumstances they find very uncomfortable. If used excessively these mechanisms lead to socially undesirable and immature behavior. Dealing with a person who is using these mechanisms, as anyone with a teenage child will say, can be challenging. Often it will appear that the person is twisting reality to suit their agenda. Immature defense mechanisms can be used by people with severe depression or a personality disorder. When someone relies exclusively on immature defenses there is an increased risk that they will develop some form of mental illness. Immature defenses include:

a) Acting out.

b) Fantasy.

c) Idealization.

d) Projection and projective identification

e) Passive aggression.

f) Somatization.

4.5 Neurotic defenses

Neurotic defenses are common in adults as they provide short-term advantages in dealing with problems.

However, if they are our primary way of dealing with issues, they can cause long-term problems in relationships, in the work environment and when it comes to enjoying life.

It is common to see these mechanisms appear in the training environment. Where we have been confronted with facts that challenge our world-view or when pressure starts to accumulate, we may resort to these mechanisms. Neurotic defenses include:

a) Displacement.

b) Dissociation.

c) Isolation.

d) Intellectualization.

e) Rationalization.

f) Minimization

g) Regression.

h) Repression.

i) Undoing.

j) Withdrawal.

4.6 Mature defense mechanisms

The 'mature' defense mechanisms are based on an accurate understanding of reality and tend to be more constructive and adaptive in nature than the other mechanisms and using them may work to address problems. While they are the most constructive of the defense mechanisms, implementing them effectively on a daily basis, can be difficult. We are more likely to be aware when we are using mature defense mechanisms, and they are commonly found in emotionally mature adults. If we rely on mature defense mechanisms, we are generally more content in ourselves and with others. These mechanisms can give us a sense of control over our environment and allow us to deal with conflicting emotions or thoughts. Malone et al. (2013) theorized that mature defense mechanisms allow us to better control stress and to maintain a much closer connection with reality. This leads to greater levels of success in work and relationships and to maintain our mental health. More effective encounters occur as a result of having the ability to use the right defense mechanism in a given context. However, overuse of these defenses is counter-productive as is using them in the wrong context. Mature defense mechanisms include:

a) Altruism.

b) Anticipation.

c) Humor.

d) Identification.

e) Introjection.

f) Sublimation.

g) Suppression.

4.7 Cognitive distortions

In 1976, the psychologist Aaron Beck first proposed a theory relating to cognitive distortions (Beck, 1976) and in the 1980s, David Burns was responsible for popularizing the idea, giving common names and examples for the distortions (Burns, 2012). More of a step-sibling than a country cousin, cognitive distortions are nevertheless closely related to defense mechanisms in both the purpose they serve and the way they function. Cognitive distortions are exactly what their name implies: they are distortions in our cognition. Simply put, they are ways that our mind convinces us of something that isn't accurate. They consist of irrational thoughts and beliefs, that we unknowingly reinforce over time. They are so subtle in their nature that it is difficult for us to recognize we are using them.

Cognitive distortions come in many forms, but they all have some things in common with each other:

- They are patterns of thinking or believing.

- They are habitual.

- They are false or inaccurate.

- They lead people to interpret the world in an irrational and maladaptive way.

- They have the potential to cause psychological damage.

One of the things that makes cognitive distortions so damaging, is that like defense mechanisms, we don't realize we are using them. They are difficult to recognize and something that is difficult to recognize is something that is difficult to change. They can lead to self-destructive behavior, such as rejecting support that is offered, not eating, not taking medication, drinking excessively, and self-harming. Cognitive distortions are closely linked with mental health problems such as depression.

In a similar vein to defense mechanisms, there are numerous cognitive distortions. These are the main ones:

1. *Filtering.* We take the negative details of an event and magnify them while filtering out all positive aspects of a situation. For instance, a person may pick out a single, unpleasant detail and dwell on it exclusively, so that their vision of reality becomes distorted. We focus exclusively on the most negative and upsetting features of a situation, removing all the positive aspects. Example: We undertake a presentation at work which is complimented and praised by ninety-five percent of the team - but we chose to dwell on the five percent of negative feedback

2. *Polarized Thinking.* Sometimes referred to as 'Black and White' or 'All or Nothing' thinking, with polarized thinking, things are seen as being black or white.; there is no grey, no middle ground. We place people or situations in "either/or" categories. If our performance falls short of perfect, we see ourselves as a total failure. These types of thoughts are characterized by terms such as or 'every', 'always', or 'never' and it is generally the negative perspective that we endorse, Example: If we get 95% in an exam, we feel like we failed.

3. *Overgeneralization.* With overgeneralization, we come to a conclusion about something, based

upon a single incident or a single piece of evidence. If something bad happens once, we then expect it to happen again and again, and we view it as a sign that now everything else will go wrong. Example: If we fail to get a job we have applied for, we think we will never get a job.

4. *Jumping to Conclusions.* If we are the type of person who jumps to conclusions, we think we know what a person is feeling or why they are acting in a certain way, without having any evidence to support our theories. We make negative interpretations or predictions even though there is nothing to support our conclusion. In particular, we believe we can determine how people are feeling toward us. This type of thinking involves two aspects:

a) Mind-reading – assuming the thoughts and intentions of others. Example: We are at a conference and have regrets about our choice of clothing, so we conclude: 'Everyone is laughing at me.'

b) Fortune-telling – anticipating the worse and treating it as fact. We are going to take an exam and 'We know for sure, we are going to fail.'

5. *Catastrophizing.* When we think catastrophically, we are unable to see any other outcome other than the worse one, however unlikely this result may be. We expect disaster to strike, at any time. When we hear about a problem, we use what 'if' questions e.g., "What if it happens to me?" Catastrophizing can have two opposing forms:

a) Maximizing – we exaggerate the importance of negative events and maximize any criticism of us.

b) Minimizing – we minimize the importance of positive events and minimize any praise we receive.

6. *Personalization.* When we believe that everything others do or say has some kind of direct, personal relevance to us, personalization is taking place. We tend to think the world revolves around us! With personalization we are also likely to continuously compare ourselves to others, trying to determine who is smarter, or funnier, or better at their job, etc. Another form of personalization occurs when we automatically assume responsibility and blame for negative events, even if they were not under our control.

In the training environment, if we tend to personalize things, then any criticism offered, even if it's constructive, feels like it is a direct personal attack upon us. We fail to recognize that the critique is on part of our work, and not on us, as a person. Any criticism causes us anxiety and makes us defensive. It may only take one piece of critique to provoke a reaction with any subsequent critique serving to escalate the feeling that its personal. [This is regularly encountered in learning environments and should be addressed as soon as it appears.]

7. *Control Fallacies.* There are two types of control fallacy:

a) External locus of control: When we tend to

blame others or circumstances for our mistakes, we are using an external locus of control fallacy. This is the tendency to believe that we are not responsible for anything and any success someone achieves is based upon luck, not effort. If we resort to this distortion, we take on a victim mentality.

b) Internal locus of control: When we have an internal locus of control, we believe that we are responsible for what happens in our life and that success is based upon the amount of effort that is expended. However, the downside of this distortion is that we tend to take responsibility for anything negative that occurs around us, regardless of the fact that we could have had no bearing on it: 'You are upset; was it something I did?'

8. *Fallacy of Fairness.* This distortion occurs when we have an unrealistic and somewhat immature view of how life should be. We think that life should be fair and then we go through it, judging everything to see if it is 'fair' or not. Life is not fair and what happens is we begin to hold very negative views of the world.

9. *Blaming.* Blaming is about not accepting that sometimes things just happen. We are always searching for someone to blame. We want to hold other people responsible for our pain and failing that, we may end blaming our self for everything bad that happens.

10. *Shoulds and Oughts.* We know how we should behave. We know there are things we ought to do.

When we don't comply with these shoulds and oughts, we feel guilty. When other people do not behave as they should or ought, it leads to anger within us. When we tell someone else what they should or ought to do, they will feel anger, frustration and resentment towards us. Shoulds and oughts are about tying us and others, to complying with unrealistic, self-imposed rules.

11. *Emotional Reasoning.* When we assume feelings are the same as fact, regardless of the evidence we are using emotional reasoning. Just because we believe that what we are feeling must be true, doesn't mean that it is true. Such thoughts are likely to be turned inward with negative consequences. When something happens and we feel stupid, does not mean that we are stupid. This type of thinking leads to self-fulfilling prophecies, where our negative thoughts end up bringing about the negative behavior we foresaw. 'I am ugly, so what is the point in making effort with my appearance.'

12. *Fallacy of Change.* We need people to change because all our hopes seem to depend on them. We put ourselves in a position where we expect that if we put a bit of pressure on them, they will change to suit us. Of course, they don't.

13. *Global Labeling.* This occurs when instead of describing a specific behavior in a person, we place a highly emotive and negative label on them that leaves no room for discussion. Instead of describing an error in the context of a specific situation we make a global judgement. For example:

if someone in a meeting has disagreed with us, we may say: 'He's an asshole.' In this we judge him in his entirety and not in relation to the circumstances of the meeting. We will do the same thing in judging ourselves. Just because we failed a course does not make us a 'loser'. Global labeling is an extreme form of 'all or nothing' thinking or 'overgeneralization'. Another form of this process is mislabeling, where we describe a set of circumstances in a highly tainted way. Instead of saying that a working parent leaves their child with a 'child-minder', we say that they leave their child with some 'random stranger just so they can make more money.'

14. *Always Being Right.* If we feel we always need to be right, we find ourselves in a position that we always need to prove it. We cannot conscience the idea that our beliefs or actions are incorrect, and we will go to any length to demonstrate the contrary. Being right is more important than the negative feelings it generates for us or the others around us.

15. *Heaven's Reward Fallacy.* In everything we do we expect our sacrifice and self-denial to be noticed and to pay off. We think that other people are going to notice what we have done and reward us for it. However, when this doesn't happen, we are left feeling disconsolate or angry.

4.8 Overcoming defense mechanisms

Recognizing the harm that the inappropriate use of

defense mechanisms can bring about is important because it means we can take measures to reduce our use of the wrong ones in the wrong circumstances. Psychologists call the method of overcoming defense mechanisms 'defense work'. Defense work is a central part of what is known as Intensive Short-Term Dynamic Psychotherapy (ISTDP). According to Davanloo (2000) there are four steps in the defense work process:

1. Identification and awareness of the defense use. In this step we observe our behavior over a period with the intention of identifying what situations bring about or trigger the use of defense mechanisms. We try and recognize patterns in our behavior and how we are feeling when we deploy them. We also want to find out which specific mechanisms we are relying on and label them correctly.

2. Clarification of the defense. In this step in we seek to clarify the purpose of the defense. This is about categorizing what specific benefit we are getting from it. Every defense has a benefit and it is important to recognize what that benefit is. It may not be the same benefit for each person.

3. Examining the consequence of the defense. In this step we look at the negative consequences of our use of the defense. Often, we will have failed to see the issues that have arisen as a result of how we have been using a defense mechanism. If we fail to recognize the negative consequences or deny their existence, this behavior is probably motivated by a reluctance to recognize or acknowledge the existence of an underlying

problem. Ironically, another defense mechanism may be at play.

4. Turning against the defense. In this step we try to stop using the defense. This can require a lot of effort and we will not succeed every time, especially if we have relied on it since childhood. This should not be viewed as failure. Recognition of what has happened is progress particularly in the early stages.

While this may seem like a simple enough process, often the reason we use some of these defense mechanisms is rooted in trauma, particularly childhood trauma and is very hard to shift. Our use of defense mechanisms is merely self-medicating. If we want to reduce the harm that defense mechanisms cause, it is the underlying trauma that first needs to be treated. This is not to say that there is not benefit in reducing our use of inappropriate defense mechanisms if that is all we do.

By understanding each of the defense mechanisms and having the ability to comprehend when and why we are using them, allows us to gain better control over them. In doing so we are more likely to use them correctly and avoid destructive behaviors.

4.9 Conclusion

Defense mechanisms are a part of normal functioning. They are instinctive. However, they can be used as a sort of psychological painkiller and like most painkillers they have addictive qualities. If we have become 'addicted' in childhood, they are going to be much more difficult to shift. Furthermore, the rigid or over-use of defense mechanisms, particularly the lower level defense mechanisms are a strong indicator of underlying mental health issues.

Defense mechanisms are not the only thing we use to avoid pain; cognitive distortions bring another raft of tactics all of which have substantial downsides. Despite the downsides many of us are still prone to use them.

Acknowledging it is difficult to stop using both defense mechanisms and cognitive distortions, in the next chapter we will look at how we can deal with pain in more effective ways.

5 - COPING

"If you are distressed by anything external, the pain is not due to the thing itself, but to your estimate of it; and this you have the power to revoke at any moment."

Meditations - Marcus Aurelius

5.1 Introduction

In the past few chapters we have spent some time explaining the problems with defense mechanisms and the associated mental health issues. In this chapter we will explore some of the things we can do to maintain our mental health and that will help us function more contently in everyday life. While many of the tips given here are relatively easy to implement none of them is a substitute for therapy. As we have already mentioned defense mechanisms often have their roots deeply planted within past traumas. Their existence may be hard to see and their causes harder to face. It is only through seeking professional help from a qualified mental health professional that one can hope to address these issues. The word qualified used here has significance – there are many people out there claiming to provide counselling services with little or no real knowledge of how the brain works. Addressing mental health issues requires us finding a person that has both the professional knowledge and is also right for us - someone we feel comfortable talking to about uncomfortable things.

5.2 Coping strategies

As we have already established to deal with stress, people use both conscious behaviors and unconscious mechanisms. Before looking at what coping strategies we can use, let's see what differentiates between them and defense mechanisms.

Coping strategies are often confused and interchanged with defense mechanisms due to their similarities. Both processes are activated in times of adversity and both reduce the arousal of negative emotions. They are adaptational processes, i.e. processes by which we are better suited to survive by taking in new information, forming new ideas or changing existing ones, and adapting our behaviors to deal with what is happening. Both processes attempt to return us to the psychological state we were in before the pain. But let us look at the differences.

Defense mechanisms:

- Occur without conscious effort and without conscious awareness.
- Occur without conscious intentionality.
- Are instinctive.
- Are selected subconsciously by the person; the person doesn't select a particular mechanism.
- Are more stable within a person and are habitual. i.e. they are enduring characteristics of a person.
- Are rigid in their application.
- Have a goal to reduce anxiety not to solve the cause.

- Function to change an internal psychological state but may have no effect on external reality.
- May result in the distortion of reality.

Coping strategies:

- Require a conscious, purposeful effort.
- Are carried out with the intent of managing or solving a problem situation.
- Allow for full control in choosing which strategy to use.
- Can be changed mid-stream; a person can choose to stop a coping strategy if it's not working and choose another instead.
- Are dependent on timing and situational factors, while personality dispositions are unimportant in determining which coping strategy a person will choose.
- Allow flexibility.
- Are reality based.
- Allow the person to achieve goals by using available resources whilst adhering to societal norms.
- Are about problem solving.
- Can be developed as a skill and will change over time.

The use of one way of dealing with stress does not exclude the simultaneous use of another. We can use both coping strategies and defense mechanisms at the same time.

5.3 Types of coping

It can be said that there are two types of coping:

1. Reactive coping. With reactive coping a stressor appears, and we react in a way we believe will help us deal with it. As the stressful event has already taken place, reactive coping is intended to compensate for the loss or alleviate the amount of harm.

2. Proactive coping. With proactive coping we aim to anticipate potential pain and act in advance either to prevent it happening or to remove its impact

Having the ability to cope in a reactive way is important but being proactive in our approach is better. Coping strategies develop from childhood and are learnt by watching others and through trial and error. How effective these are, depends upon which strategy we choose, but also on our belief that the chosen strategy will work. This is referred to as coping self-efficacy.

While psychologists disagree on the specific classification of coping strategies that are available, there are three common forms of strategy that are recognized. These are:

1. Appraisal-Focused Strategies: These strategies attempt to modify the thought processes that are associated with pain. This can be done in two ways. Either we try to alter the way we are thinking about the problem by reframing it, or we change our relevant goals or values.

2. Problem-Focused Strategies: These strategies try to deal with the cause of the problem. We try to change or eliminate the cause of the pain by analyzing it and developing the skills necessary to deal with it.

3. Emotion-Focused Strategies: These strategies focus on the feelings associated with the problem rather than the problem itself. We attempt to change the emotions we are feeling about it by managing our mental state.

A person will employ a mixture of all these strategies when attempting to cope with stress/pain. We will now examine several of the most helpful coping strategies.

5.4 Health management

We need to be proactive in managing our health for two coping related reasons:

1. Poor health or worries about are health are a major cause of stress and can be very easily triggered. Once triggered they can easily spiral out of control.

2. Good physical health provides a sound foundation for good mental health. Furthermore, good physical health helps us deal much better with physical pain.

Areas of health management that help us cope with pain include:

- Sleep. If we aren't getting enough sleep our physical and mental well-being will deteriorate rapidly. The average person needs about 7-8 hours of sleep per night. The quality of sleep is important and will be affected by caffeine and alcohol intake. The amount of light and amount of sound entering the room will affect the sleep process. Sleep cleansing is a process designed to improve the quality of sleep. It is about preparing the brain for sleep mentally and physically. It includes avoiding electronic devices, the light of which activates the brain, and clearing the mind of the day's troubles, acknowledging them, but consciously deciding to deal with them in the morning.

- Eating properly. There is a correlation between the type of food we eat and how we feel mentally. This also relates to the quantity of food we eat. Poor food choices lead to poor mental health.

- Physical activity. Exercise or playing sports contribute to good mental health. A fast pace run at the end of the day can help alleviate a lot of stress. A brisk walk in the outdoors will also make a positive contribution. Making exercise a routine helps us create a good baseline for mental well-being.

- Healthy sexual relationships. Sexual relationships are a normal part of human behavior. Including both the physical enjoyment and the sense of intimacy they bring, helps us to be in a healthy state of mind. For some people the lack of such relationships can create a sense of frustration and/or damage to self-worth.

5.5 Resilience

Resilience is the ability to manage stress, to cope positively with it, to keep going when things get tough and to bounce back from things that have gone wrong. It is also about achieving our goals despite challenging circumstances. It is a set of skills which can be learned and includes:

- Self-awareness – the ability to pay attention to our thoughts, emotions, behaviors, and psychological reactions. (See below.)
- Self-regulation – the ability to change our thoughts, emotions, and behavior, to meet changing circumstances.
- Mental agility – the ability to look at situations from different perspectives and to think creatively and flexibly.
- Affiliation – the ability to build and maintain strong, trusting relationships. (See below.)
- Self-efficacy – the ability to focus on what we can control, and to have confidence in our abilities.
- Acceptance – the ability to accept change in our circumstances and accepting there are some things we cannot change (See below.)

5.6 Self-awareness

Be more self-aware. One key benefit of understanding defense mechanisms is the knowledge that they work on an unconscious level. To put it more plainly, we go through life doing a lot of things that we don't know we are doing, and we do them often when we really should be thinking about what we are doing i.e. when we are feeling pain. It is our unconscious mind that reacts to any type of pain, physical or mental. Our brain reacts to mental pain in a similar manner to us pulling our hand away from a hot object – instantaneously and without thought. The purpose in being more self-aware is to curtail any negative effects that this reaction may have; we cannot stop a reaction.

Few of us know how we come across to other people particularly when we are under pressure or reacting to stress. Part of being more self-aware is to make a conscious effort to note our behavior when we know we are under 'attack'.

To have a clearer understanding of how we are when under attack, we first need to know how we are as an emotional baseline. We can do this when we have a moment to ourselves. We will have to do it a few times because our baseline mood can vary from day-to-day. These are the sort of questions we can ask:

- How am I feeling physically? A quick head-to-toe mental body scan helps answer this.
- How do I feel about my life?
- How does my future look? Consider short, medium and longer terms.
- How are my relationships?
- Do I have any issues of pressing importance?
- Do I have unresolved matters affecting my mental state?
- Are my expectations about myself or life in general, accurate and realistic?

These types of question help us establish what our

baseline emotional state is. We can view our state across three broad continuums:

1. Well-being or malaise.

2. Calm or tense.

3. Pain or pleasure.

Once we have a reasonable sense of our baseline emotional state, we can start to analyze how we behave when we find ourselves in a situation where someone is frustrating us. Here are a few things to note:

- Physical condition. Is my breathing more rapid or deeper? Can I feel my heart-rate? Do I feel a tensing of my muscles?

- Voice. Is my voice raised? Is my speech more rapid? What tone of voice am I using?

- Words used and sentence structure. What words have I used? How did I construct my sentence?

- Content. Is what I have just said factually correct? Have I added or removed detail?

- Reaction. How are other people reacting to my behavior? What am I seeing in their faces? What are their replies? Has their voice tone changed?

- It can help to keep a journal or notebook detailing what we find and then analyzing it at regular intermissions.

Adulthood is a time for reassessing the assumptions of our formative years that have often resulted in distorted views of reality. It is worth taking the time to think about our childhood events and expectations and where they now sit with our adult life. A significant amount of the destructive use of defense mechanisms, often stems from childhood issues.

Gaining a better sense of who we are and how we behave allows us to make changes where changes are needed. We also need to learn to accept who we are. There are bits we like and bits we can improve. If we find that the way we deal with pain, creates more pain, then we can start to work on that.

5.7 Affiliation

Interaction with others is a basic human need and very helpful in managing stress. We benefit from the company of others and their counsel can be helpful in allowing us to see a problem in a different, more objective, light. Interactions can provide opportunities to vocalize how we are feeling, and they can create distractions, to take our minds away from a problem.

Affiliation can come in many forms including being involved in community activities or spending quality time with our partner. Different problems may be helped by interaction with different people. If the cause of our pain is our partner, then sharing with a work colleague may help and if the pain originates at work place then sharing with our partner may be appropriate. It's good to talk.

5.8 Acceptance

A big step in making life a better place to be, is having the ability to tolerate unpleasant emotions and to accept unpleasant situations and people. If we can learn to tolerate feelings of anger, frustration, fear, and sadness we are more likely to create the mental space needed to find solutions to what is troubling us. But doing, is not as easy as saying. Situations are frustrating and people are annoying. Here are a few tips:

- Respect people and the choices they make.
- Forgive.
- Be more open-minded.
- Seek different views and experiences.
- Be patient.
- Accept uncertainty.

Tolerance is the exercise of deliberately allowing thoughts of something, of which we disapprove. It is about adopting a fair and objective attitude toward those whose opinions or practices, differ from ours. While most of the time we flee from even thinking about such things, one way to develop greater tolerance is to take the time to think about a topic we find repugnant. While we hold that idea in our mind, we try to analyze how we feel about it and why we feel that way. While doing so we can note any physical changes within us and find ways to overcome those feelings.

When we are struggling to tolerate what is happening, there are often indicators present that foreshadow what is to come. These may be very subtle and if we are not practiced in looking for them, they will go unnoticed. They may start with slight discomfort and a sense that things are not going the way we want. We may start to fidget, shuffling in our seat, unable to get comfortable. Our physical demeanor is reflecting our mental state. We find ourselves gripping our pen or grinding our teeth. We can feel the anger rising from our gut. Then we spew…

And what comes out is our pain in one form or another. Remember: There may be a perverse pleasure in just letting the venom fly. We may have the misguided view that 'It's what we do and who we are.' There is comfort in the familiar.

By paying attention when the irritation or discomfort starts, we have a better chance of gaining control over them. To do so we need to turn our focus inward and recognize what is going on inside of us. The main thing here is to stop the escalating story we are telling ourselves namely: 'This is annoying. This is wrong. This really pisses me off.' We can then concentrate on bringing our feelings under control with a counter narrative. There may be a huge temptation to try and change the circumstances or the other person's view. Changing something is the opposite of accepting it and it is not what we are trying to do. As we get more and more practice at attending to what is going on inside of us and in taking countermeasures, the feelings of anxiety or frustration will pass. Recognize when feelings are starting to spiral up and make a conscious effort to spiral them back down again.

Accepting things that we don't like can be helped by self-talk:

- I see what is happening and much as I don't like it, I am going to tolerate it.
- I don't like this; it is uncomfortable, but I have survived a lot worse.
- I know my flaws. I accept them.
- Not long to go; it will soon be over.
- I know what I am feeling; it is normal for me when this happens.

There will be many times when we encounter dis-comfort in our life. The more often we expose ourselves to it and deal with it the less power it will have over us. So, while we may not quite want to embrace discomfort, we can at least hold hands for a while.

5.9 Exposure therapy and habituation

If we have identified things that cause us to react in a negative way, then we can take steps to addressing them. There are two interlinked methods of helping us deal better with stress and pain, exposure theory (McNally, 2007) and habituation.

Exposure therapy works a bit like a vaccination; we are exposed to the stimuli in a limited way which then protects us when we are exposed to it in a major way. It works by exposing us to a series of gradually increasing stress-inducing situations. These exposures allow us to understand what is occurring both cognitively and emo-tionally, and to practice coping strategies. The therapy commences in a controlled environment, then later with exposure to the stimuli, in real world situations. Expo-sure therapy involves breaking a pattern of negative re-sponse. It works by changing the type of activity in the areas of our brain which are responsible for keeping us safe, including the amygdala and the hippocampus.

Exposure therapy is effective in treating disorders such as phobias and post-traumatic stress disorder (PTSD). One of the main symptoms with PTSD is the avoidance of things that trigger it. As a result, the sufferer avoids encountering ordinary cues in life and the avoid-ance maintains the PTSD. Exposure therapy treats this by presenting the cues in a controlled environment, so we become habituated to them. Exposure therapy has the added benefit of developing self-efficacy; we come to the realization that we are capable of confronting feelings of fear and overcoming them.

Habituation is a form of learning in which a person (or any other organism) decreases or ceases their responses to stimuli, after repeated or prolonged presentations of those stimuli. Key elements of the habituation process include:

- Duration: If the habituation stimulus is not presented for a long enough period before a sudden reintroduction, the response will once again reappear.

- Frequency: The more frequently the stimulus is presented to the patient the faster habituation will occur.

- Intensity: Very intense stimuli tend to result in slower habituation. In some cases, habituation is impossible.

- Change: Changing the intensity or duration of the stimulation may result in a reoccurrence of the original response.

- No reward or punishment: There is no reward or consequence for the patient when they are exposed to the stimulus.

- A learned adaptation: With habituation the patient learns to adapt to the repeated presentation of a stimulus. It does not mean that their ability to sense the stimuli or to physically respond to it is reduced.

In exposure therapy there are two types of habituation

1. Within-session habituation. This occurs when fear decreases during a therapy session as exposure is conducted.

2. Between-session habituation. This occurs when fear decreases between therapy sessions.

There is a down side to habituation: it is the same process as causes us to take others for granted. Remember when every little aspect of our partner used to thrill us because it was new and exciting, but now we don't even notice - that's habituation.

5.10 Time management

We put a lot of pressure on ourselves because we do not manage our time properly. Pressure leads to stress. We may delude ourselves with comments like: 'I work better under pressure.' or 'I am more focused nearer the time.' The reality is that while there may be some truth, for some of us, in this type of comment, more often we are in denial. Furthermore, all it takes is some minor crisis to arise and everything goes 'to hell in a handcart'. Putting in place simple time management strategies give us the breathing space to cope more effectively when painful events arise.

5.11 Assertiveness

Communication exists on a continuum, which ranges from passive acceptance to responding with aggression. Assertiveness is about finding the middle ground. When we are assertive, we emphasize our needs in a manner that is direct and unequivocal but respectful of the needs of others. In being assertive we seek to find the balance and we listen when we are being spoken to. While assertiveness may seem a simple concept, putting it into practice requires a lot of social skill including the ability to interpret situations correctly and self-confidence to select and utilize an appropriate response. Being assertive is a very helpful coping strategy because it means we can articulate our emotions and concerns in a non-conflicting and rational way.

5.12 Seeing the 'big picture'

Life is full of small frustrations, each of which has the possibility to undermine our mental well-being. Small frustrations aggregated can lead us to boiling point. By knowing what the big picture is in each aspect of our life and by focusing on these, we can avoid a lot of stress. Furthermore, if we recognize that there are many small boring steps to be made towards our goals, we are likely to be more accepting of these necessary steps and more patient with our progress.

5.13 Coping with anger

Anger is driven by other underlying emotions including feelings of being frustrated, feelings of disgust, feelings of irritation and by feelings that things are out of our control. Anger is primarily driven by the more primitive part of our brain and is a safety motivated response. It can arise as a result of several small steps over a prolonged period or be instantaneous. It is destructive in its nature. Dealing with anger is not easy and if we find ourselves reacting angrily on a regular basis it is worthwhile seeking professional help to try and identify the causes of our anger and addressing them. In the short-term, we can try some of these options:

- Ten second rule. Count to ten (slowly before replying). This allows us to ground our emotional brain and let the rational brain take control.

- Tell me why you think that. Ask the person gently to explain why they think what they have just said, telling them that it is so you can understand them better. This allows us to hear any nuances in what they are saying and gives us time to regain composure.

- 24-hour rule. If we feel annoyed about something, if we can leave it for 24 hours before responding, leave it for 24 hours. A lot of the heat will have gone out of the situation.

- Take a 'time out.' Just say 'Stop' then go for a walk or move to a quiet place. This lets us gather our thoughts.

- Keep an anger log. Writing down times when we were angry and the circumstances at play at the time can help us identify underlying issues. It also allows us to accurately identify what we were feeling and excise those feelings.

- Stick to the 'I' word. By keeping a conversation in terms of 'I' means that we remain in our frame of reference. It focuses on how we are feeling and is therefore less accusatory. Accusatory lan-

guage, such as the use of the pronoun 'you', escalates conflict.

- The 'really' rule. Just say: 'Really.' Nothing more
  and in a neutral tone. This hands the next move
  back to the other person and allows our brain
  time to process.

These techniques are neither full proof, nor easy to
implement. We are trying to regain control of instinctive
behavior. All need practice but even if we have reacted
initially, we should implement them as soon as we can,
rather than allowing the situation to escalate.

5.14 Breathing

One of the simplest methods of coping with a stressful situation and one which will bring immediate results
is that of taking prolonged deep breaths. We take a deep
breath in through our nose, hold it for a count of five
and then release it. We do this, five or six times in a row.
This technique can be very beneficial in controlling anger. Other breathing techniques are useful in lowering
anxiety and are well worth researching and learning.

5.15 Reframing

Reframing is a technique used by psychologists to
help create a different way of looking at a situation, person, or relationship and so changing its meaning. The
idea behind it is that what we see depends on the frame
through which we see it. Just as adjusting the lens on a
camera changes what is seen in a picture, reframing
changes how something is perceived. In essence, reframing is saying: 'Don't view it as that; view it like this. For

example: We may be disappointed because we have failed to obtain a promotion at work: 'I am sad I didn't get the job.' We can reframe this in a way: 'I will be able to spend more time with my family.' The picture is the same, we have just changed how we are looking at it.

If we find ourselves annoyed about what someone is saying or doing, with reframing we can step back from what is being said and done, and consider the frame, or lens through which we are viewing it. By understanding the unspoken assumptions, that are present and taking cognizance of them we may be able to form a more accurate meaning of the event. For example: We may believe that a person is shouting at us because they are angry with us, but by reframing it, we can see the origin of the anger is not us, but the circumstances.

5.16 Mindfulness

Another effective coping strategy is the use of 'mindfulness'. Much has been written on the topic and unfortunately much of it is pretentious drivel. However, it is a valuable technique to know for coping with pain. Taking the time to research and apply the theory will pay dividends. Mindfulness has its origins in Eastern meditation practices but has been proven in clinical studies to have substantial physical and mental health benefits.

Mindfulness (Gotink et al., 2016) is the process of focusing our attention on what is occurring in the present moment. The goal with mindfulness is merely to become a conscious self-observer. We are not trying to solve problems merely acknowledging they exist. Mindfulness involves paying attention in a way that is composed of three elements:

1. Being present in the moment.

2. Being purposeful in what we are doing.

3. Thinking without judgment.

Mindfulness makes us more aware of our thoughts, behaviors, emotions and motivations. In turn, this allows us to manage them more effectively.

5.17 Self-affirmation

Self-affirmation theory focuses on how people adapt to information or experiences that threaten their self-esteem (Steele 1988). The theory holds that if we take the time to think about values that are personally relevant to us, we are less likely to experience anxiety and react defensively, when we are confronted with circumstances that contradicts or threatens our sense of self.

Self-affirmation involves building up a reservoir of positive feelings. A lot of the time we fail to acknowledge the good feelings stemming from kind things people have said about us or things that have gone well in our homeplace or in work. By building up these memories we create the knowledge that when things are bad, they will not always be. One of the ways we can develop a stronger more positive sense of self is by vocalizing our achievements in the form of self-affirming statements. The more often we tell ourselves these things, the more likely we are to believe them:

- I have managed a successful project.

- I submitted a good piece of work

- I had a good meeting with….

- I had a good holiday.

- I had a very relaxing weekend.

- I was kind to that person.

5.18 Other activities

There are many other activities that help us build a solid baseline for mental well-being. While some may sound somewhat quaint, all are known to help with mental health. They include:

- Having hobbies. Hobbies divert our interest from reality and allow us to focus on something we enjoy thus excluding, albeit for a time, stressors.

- Getting out in fresh air and enjoying natural surroundings. Nature settles the mind. Even time spent in a garden has a positive effect.

- Yelling in a safe place can alleviate frustration. Throwing eggs at a wall also works!

- Read, to both expand your knowledge and to relax. Novels can make for a great escape.

- Create, make or build something. For example: Coloring books for adults have become very popular because the act of creation helps our cognitive abilities refocus onto other things, diminishing the pain that emanates from stress.

- Listen to music. Music can have a profound effect on the brain.

- Play with an animal. Regular time with a pet can have a very positive aspect on our mental health. Walking someone else's dog can be an easy way to reap the benefit.

- Find a tree and hug it[6].

5.19 Conclusion

An important part of our ability as adults to function effectively, is our ability to know which coping strategy to use and when to use it. If we have a sound understanding of reality, we are less likely to misjudge events and/or resort to the use of inappropriate ways of dealing with negative events. However, if we have a distorted view of reality and we are less circumspect in the methods we choose to deal with adversity then this will likely result in more conflict and less happiness.

Everything we have discussed in this chapter is about giving us a better chance of dealing with the ups and downs of life in a more constructive way. If we don't learn and practice these strategies, then we will be left with nothing to rely on other than our defense mechanisms, and that is probably not going to work out well for us.

---

[6] This doesn't really work. It's just using humor as a defense mechanism to deal with the boredom that sets in when writing.

6 – LEARNING AND DEVELOPMENT

"What don't change, can't learn."
Granny Weatherwax

Lords and Ladies - Terry Pratchett

6.1 Introduction

In this chapter we will look how defense mechanisms come into play in an educational setting. When we use the term 'student' we are referring to an adult learner and how they may feel or react. When we use the term 'educator', we are referring to the person responsible for managing the class, for example: a teacher or trainer. The terms 'we' and 'our' will be used to refer to us, as educators and how we may be feeling or behaving.

If an adult has had trauma free development from birth, then it is unlikely that defense mechanisms will be a major problem for the educator. However, it is rare to find a class where this is the case for all students.

An understanding of the defense mechanisms is important to us as educators, for two reasons:

1. To be aware of our own defenses so that we can guard against the way they will affect the teaching process if we feel threatened by issues that arise including those with students. If we are not in control of our defense mechanisms, they will

take control of us as soon as we feel pressured. This can happen easily where students will always out-number us and where they may resent what we are saying. If, as educators, we don't use situationally appropriate defense mechanisms, in a controlled manner, we are likely to:

a) Exacerbate any already difficult situation.

b) Cause ourselves psychological harm.

c) Injure the feelings of the students.

2. To be sensitive and respectful of a student's defense mechanisms which emerge when they feel threatened by what is happening in the class. The educator needs to be able to recognize which defense mechanism is at play and then search for ways to overcome the challenge it has created.

6.2 Identifying defense mechanisms at play

There are several ways that will help us recognize when defense mechanisms are being used and which defense mechanism is being used:

1. Know the warning signs. To be able to identify indicators we must know what those indicators are, and we must know them well enough that we recognize them in an instant.

2. Avoid jumping to conclusions. One swallow does not make a summer. Just because we see an indicator that a defense mechanism may be at play, does not mean it is. We need to look for a pattern of behavior – different indicators, at different times and in different circumstances.

3. Listen. The most effective way to identify when and which defense mechanism is being used is to listen to the words the person is using. Unless we listen properly, we have little chance of accurately identifying what is occurring. This is the reason psychologists put us in a chair and let us do the talking. Listening is a skill, few of us have bothered to learn and even fewer of us regularly apply. The techniques involved in good listening are captured in the concept referred to as 'active listening'.

6.3 Active listening

Here are a few tips about how to listen more effectively:

- Take time. Listening to someone takes time; if we are in a rush we won't be listening.
- Avoid distractions. If there is a lot going on around us, or we have a lot of competing issues in our head, we won't be able to listen. Turn off the phone!
- Be present. We need to be present in the moment: 'I am here to listen to this person. Nothing else is as important now.'
- Listen to the words. If we can't repeat the last four words that the person has said, we have not listened.
- Listen to the voice tone and speed of speech. Approximately 40% of what we are saying comes from the way we say it. Change an intonation and we change the meaning.

- Observe the non-verbal communication. Approximately 50% of communication is conveyed non-verbally through facial and body movements and through the accompanying gestures. Miss these and we miss the meaning.
- Listen to hear not to formulate a reply. We all tend to listen to half of what the person is saying then start formulating how we will reply.
- Listen for the facts and feelings. We want to know what has happened (facts) and the person's emotions about them (feelings).

6.4 Dispositional barriers to learning

There are three types of barrier to learning that are common in an educational setting.

- Institutional barriers. These are policies, procedures, or situations that systematically disadvantage certain groups of people.
- Situational barriers. These are barriers that are created by the student's personal circumstances. They lie outside the classroom and involve things like family or work circumstances.
- Dispositional barriers. These as psychological perceptions about oneself as a learner. They are internal. Dispositional barriers include low motivation; low self-esteem, embarrassment, and fear of failure.

Dispositional barriers are more powerful barriers than are institutional or situational barriers, since dispositional barriers involve our past negative experiences and negative perceptions of ourselves and our abilities

(Merriam,1984). It is with these dispositional barriers that there will often be an interaction with defense mechanisms. When the past is still playing out in a student's head, it can be a lot more difficult to accept new learning. Breaking down these mental barriers in the unconscious is not an easy task.

If a student has a fragile ego, learning can be particularly frightening. When an educator conveys a message to the effect that: 'This is stuff you don't know. It will challenge your world view and self-image.' the student is likely to react in a defensive way. Their defense mechanisms will be used inappropriately and can create circumstances where learning is prevented or distorted.

Furthermore, it can be very difficult for a student to 'learn' that methods they have been using for prolonged periods, are considered by the educator to be ineffective, erroneous or outdated. The student will naturally try to defend the methods they have used, and that they have grown comfortable with. If, in the classroom setting the student is asked to try new things and they fail, their ego will take a hit. This bad feeling is likely to be exacerbated by the fact that other students will see the failure. This can bring on the feeling of shame. When the student begins to feel pressure, they may react by denying the fact that they are struggling, or they may minimize the extent of the problem. During exercises they may attempt to rationalize why they were unsuccessful blaming the circumstances or citing small initial errors which led to bigger mistakes. "If I hadn't misheard the first sentence everything would have been fine."

As the pressure mounts, the student may resort to more primitive defense mechanisms such as projecting the failure onto the educators. The student may question the impartiality of the educator making allegations that another student is being favorably treated or that they are being unfairly treated. They may question the knowledge or ability of the educator: "What do they know anyway?" "They didn't explain it properly." "There is no need for them to say that." With these remarks the student is trying to project blame for their own failure onto the educator, thereby protecting their self-image.

A word of warning here to training staff: be aware of how powerful and insidious projective identification is. Good educators constantly question themselves about their performance, seeking to continually improve how they teach. If someone is 'projecting' their failure on to the trainer, it can be very easy for a trainer to start to internalize the blame, which is exactly what the student wants.

In other cases, the pressure on a student becomes so great that they resort to passive aggressiveness as a defense. They begin to ask irrelevant questions. They disrupt activities in the classroom by making noise or arriving late.

If future success in the student's job is dependent on successfully completing the training that the student is struggling with, then fear can create very unpleasant feelings. Feelings of fear will escalate, and the student will adopt a defensive approach. The student may seek out other students for support. This can be relatively easy on a course where many of the students are struggling. It is not unusual for other students to rally around in support of their colleague, particularly if that person is popular, or has a charismatic disposition. A manager adopting this attitude in class can be particularly disruptive because of the influence they are likely to have on their fellow students. If a class deteriorates in this way, an almost insurmountable barrier to learning is created. We will now look at several ways we can use our understanding of defense mechanisms in a learning environment.

6.5 Problem-based learning

Problem-based learning is a teaching approach that challenges students to learn through engagement in a real problem. Rather than having an educator provide facts and then testing the student's ability to recall these facts, problem-based learning gets students to apply knowledge to new situations. Students are faced with contextualized, unstructured problems and are asked to discover solutions. Problem based learning does not focus on solving the problem presented with a defined solution, it focuses on the development of other skills including the ability to acquire relevant knowledge, teamwork, critical thinking and effective communication.

There are many advantages to students in using this approach, as it allows them to:

- Become more active in their learning as they work out which information, they need to find out in order to solve a problem.
- Develop transferable and employability skills that can be used immediately the workplace.
- Improve team working.
- Involve research and analytical skills.
- Develop debating skills.
- Develop critical thinking and creative skills.

- Improve problem-solving skills.
- Increase motivation because of their sense of involvement.
- Learn to transfer their existing knowledge to new situations.
- Develop the ability to deal with stressful situations.

In using problem-based learning we may see an increased use of defense mechanisms. This is due to feelings of frustration that may arise. This should be viewed in a positive light. Both student and educator become aware of the use of defense mechanisms and the educator can take the opportunity to explain what is happening, why it may be happening and how the defense mechanism is likely to play out in the work place.

Problem based learning is an effective way to train students to cope with high pressure roles, but this inevitably involves them coming under significant pressure during the training event. If emotional pressure is excluded the student cannot learn how to operate in such a situation and will fail in the real world, as soon as pressure arises. When students, encounter emotional issues, this is a good time to introduce coping strategies. Later in the real world, the student is more likely to use those strategies, rather than relying on defense mechanisms.

The educator must remember that problem-based learning takes time. Not all students will progress at the same speed. Sometimes it will be necessary to slow some students down, to allow the others to catch up. And some students may require more hints towards a solution than others. In allowing them to progress at a reasonable pace and under their own steam, we are not teaching them to be helpless or to fail, we are developing their self-efficacy – the belief that they can do it.

6.6 Transformative learning

New knowledge is one thing. How it is used use it another. But changing who we are, is something else again. If we are seeking long-term behavior change in our students, then what is required is that we change aspects of their value system (See Figure 2.1). If we want to be as sure as we ever can be, about how a student will perform under a given set of circumstances, then transformative learning is one tool we can use.

Transformative learning is a theory that uses disorienting dilemmas to challenge students' thinking. Students are encouraged to use critical thinking and questioning to consider if their underlying assumptions and beliefs about the world, are accurate.

Mezirow (2009) describes transformative learning as: "learning that transforms problematic frames of reference to make them more inclusive, discriminating, reflective, open, and emotionally able to change."

Mezirow believed that transformation usually resulted from a "disorienting dilemma" which was triggered by a life crisis or major life transition. It may also result from an accumulation of alterations over a period. In transformative learning these type of predicaments, can be created by an educator, with the intention of bringing about transformation.

Transformative learning involves a process of "perspective transformation". This has three elements:

1.   Psychological – changes in how we view and understand ourselves.
2.   Convictional – changes of our value system.
3.   Behavioral – changes in how we behave.

Disorientation is a central aspect of transformative learning and one which must be introduced by the educator if the learning is to take place, Getting the right level of disorientation is key. Too little and the transformation won't happen; too much and the student will withdraw or become openly aggressive. For the students, they will find themselves in a crisis like situation and one which is both unavoidable and requiring an urgent need to change. In order to 'survive', change is necessary.

Transformative learning is likely to have a profound effect on students, with some describing it as 'life changing'. In delivering this type of training the educator must know what they are trying to achieve and know exactly what they are doing. It is very likely that students will react vigorously when the disorientation occurs, with any and every defense mechanism coming into play.

6.7 Activating defenses

While to some educators it may seem a strange thing to want to do, there are two sets of circumstance where we might consider deliberately activating a student's defense mechanisms. This is a decision that needs careful consideration based on a cost benefit analysis and with a heavy ethical weighting. The two sets of circumstance are:

1.   Where it is apparent that a student's ego defense mechanisms have already created a block

to their learning and development.

2. To assess if the student has the aptitude to carry out a particular role.

Often students come to a classroom because they are struggling in the work place. They may have been referred by a manager or by their human resources department. The student may have found themselves in conflict with managers, colleagues or customers. There may be some level of concern about the way they behave in interpersonal relationships. As we have already discussed training is not always just about passing on new information, it may be about effecting long-term personal change. With a student who has a history of conflict with others and their job is in jeopardy, training can be a good place to understand what is occurring with their behavior. By putting them through scenarios or roleplays where they are under pressure, the educator can identify the ways in which the student manages their behavior. Because there is then a specific event which can be discussed, it is much easier for the educator to point out what occurred, rather than alluding to hypothetical events. It will be much 'safer' for the student to discuss what has happened with an educator, as opposed to a manager. If the educator is unable to correct the problem through training, then at least the employer has taken all reasonable steps to help the employee, and they can then make more informed decisions.

And for the student, the training will have provided them with a greater knowledge of defense mechanisms, and this should enable them to employ coping strategies or more mature defense mechanisms or at least to try and avoid the negative effects of using immature defense mechanisms. While there may be no direct harm in allowing a student to persist in using pathological or immature defense mechanisms, relying upon them means that in the longer-term the student is more likely to become frustrated or depressed and they are at greater risk of suicide. Of course, the educator can always turn a blind eye to what is happening...

The second set of circumstances relate to assessment. Designing assessment to test a student's innate abilities is simple to achieve. For example: If a student must have a certain level of fitness for the role there are numerous standardized fitness tests available. If a student must speak a foreign language, they may be asked to sit an exam. However, testing to see if a student has the aptitude to carry out certain roles is more difficult. One way this can be done is with the use of roleplays.

Effective training allows students to encounter reality-based roleplays that reflect events they are likely to encounter on completion of the training. Constructing role plays that will train a student for their job can be difficult. Assessing how the student performs during those roleplays adds another level of difficulty for the educator. When there are additional consequences at play such as a pass/fail element, then good role plays are extremely difficult to construct.

These are some of the things that should be in place for assessed roleplays to have utility and for them to be fair to students. They should:

- Be written by someone who has an expert knowledge of the role and a professional knowledge of teaching.

- Be reality based.
- Test against a limited number of criteria.
- Reflect contemporaneously the training that is being provided.
- Be assessed by educators trained in assessment.
- Be marked against agreed criteria.
- Have control measures in place to ensure fairness and consistency in marking.

The pressure created by the knowledge that it is a pass/fail situation mimics the stress that the student will encounter in real life. Often we will hear a student say: "I wouldn't have done that in the real world." or "I just can't do roleplays. Give me the real thing. I have no problems there." Defense mechanisms are at play. How a student performs in role-plays is a strong indicator as to how they will behave in real life. There are several advantages about seeing how the student behaves for the educator, the student and line managers.

The educator will know:

- If the student has the aptitude for the role.
- What additional training may benefit the student.

The student will know:

- How the type of pressure feels.
- The level and nature of the pain
- The things likely to trigger their defenses
- If they want to carry out the role.
- Strategies to cope with the pain.

Managers will know:

- The student's level of suitability for role.
- Risks that may be present in deploying the student.
- Control measures they need to implement to protect or help the student perform their tasks.

During assessment, if the educator observes that a student relies excessively on pathological or immature defense mechanisms it may well bring into question the student's suitability, at that time, for the role. What we are referring to here is not a clinical assessment of the student concerned. It is about an experienced and knowledgeable educator making a professional judgement about what is occurring with the student and their suitability for the role they are being asked to undertake. Employers have an obligation to keep workers safe and this includes psychological safety. It would not be a wise choice to ask someone to deal with the victims of childhood abuse if that person has not dealt with their own childhood abuse. Nor would it be a good choice to make someone a fire safety officer if they have not recovered from being traumatized in a previous fire.

When undertaking training of this nature, it is incumbent on the educators to have put in place control measures:

- Students attending training where there is significant psychological pressure should be warned accordingly.
- Students should be asked to identify any ongoing psychological issues they have and are aware of, prior to attending.
- There must be ready access for the students to

a mental health professional during the training. Putting students on a trapeze may be dangerous but putting students on a trapeze with no safety net, is negligence.

And for those who question whether students should be placed under the type of pressure that will bring out defense mechanisms, here are a few thoughts:

- If a student is to undertake a dangerous role is it better to know how they will react by seeing it in the classroom or by waiting until it happens in the real world?
- Would you rather learn how you will react to danger when there is someone there to step in or wait until you are alone and see how you cope?
- Crossing the road is dangerous. That's why our parents lead us across it the first few times. They put us in danger. They do it despite us being frightened but they do it in a safe way.
- "What don't change, can't learn." Change is painful! Especially if we are talking about long-term change in a person's behavior.
- Being frightened may frighten you, but for some, being frightened is a good way to learn how to deal with fear.

6.8 Teaching helplessness

Unfortunately, in many training environments, those with limited or no knowledge of psychology insist in creating environments where students are not allowed to fail, or where even creating the slightest hint of challenge is scorned. Flying under the false flag of creating a 'safe learning environment' these misguided individuals are of the belief that if a student feels any discomfort it will be detrimental to both their learning and their long-term mental health. This approach has many flaws:

- Students need to be trained for the environment they are likely to encounter in the real world. If you are going to be dealing with circumstances where people are likely to be offensive toward you, training needs to reflect that reality and students need to become habituated to the problems, they will face.

- All jobs are not the same. If you are going to be working in a world where people might try and kill you the training for it needs to prepare you to survive.

- If students are being taught to make decisions while under pressure, they are much more likely to make good decisions when they encounter pressure, if they have been trained to do so.

- The assumption is made that the student cannot think for themselves or stand up for themselves and therefore, they must always be protected. At best, this attitude is condescending but more often all it does is teach helplessness. The student comes to believe that anything they find challenging or contradictory to their views or self-image cannot be said to them. And if per chance it should happen, there will always be a knight in shining armor to come to their rescue. Hardly surprising that when released into the real world they struggle to cope and end up with mental health issues.

- Even though most of us have encountered the long-term detrimental effects that having an overly protective parent will have on a person's life, there is a failure to recognize that an overly protective educational system has the same effects.
- Clearing away anything that a student may find upsetting and protecting them from feeling unsafe means we end up teaching the students habits that are seen in people suffering from anxiety and depression.
- Constantly preparing students for danger in the classroom primes their mind to see danger even if there is none. Hardly surprising when they start to see it everywhere.

There is a big difference between keeping students physically safe and keeping them mentally 'safe'. While there are limited circumstances where students will be put at physical risk while training, it is not the same for emotional or mental safety. Unfortunately, what has happened in many learning environments is that the concept of what it takes for students to be 'safe' has been grossly expanded. Pushing the boundaries of what constitutes mental safety helps no one and hurts many. Regardless of the work we will be undertaking, in most jobs the minimum we must learn to deal with is people who have potentially offensive views. While the level of stress a student is exposed to will always take cognizance of the role the student is being trained for, as general guidance mental safety does not include:

- Being protected from discomfort or anxiety.
- Being challenged regarding behavior or views.

- Being exposed to disturbing behavior, language or images.
- Failure.

Where the purpose of adult education is to prepare students for a role they are undertaking, the educator has an obligation to ensure that the training they get prepares them physically and mentally for that role. This will inevitably involve varying degrees of discomfort and anxiety. While the training should always be adapted to meet the audience, it is not the case of adopting a lowest common denominator position. And then wrapping all the students in cotton wool.

Being kind and gentle may seem a commendable approach, but the world is not kind and gentle. We need to teach our students to survive.

6.9 Dunning-Kruger effect

One of the purposes of this book is to identify when defense mechanisms are likely to come into play in the learning environment. As we have already discussed defense mechanisms are there in part to protect our sense of self-esteem, our ego. Justin Kruger and David Dunning (1999) postulated a theory that has become known as the 'Dunning-Kruger effect'. It goes like this: people who are incompetent and lack knowledge in a field tend to massively overestimate their abilities because, quite simply, they don't know enough to recognize what they don't know. In slightly more unkind words: 'Some people are too stupid to realize how stupid they are.' Many of us will recognize this effect at play in managers we have had the misfortune of working for.

To a greater or lesser extent, we are all guilty of this at times. we repeatedly and consistently fool ourselves into thinking we know more about a topic than we do, and so convince ourselves we have nothing more to learn. This leads us to making poor decisions because we have blinded ourselves to other evidence. In addition, our false confidence in our own beliefs prevents us from learning.

This effect will also be seen in the classroom with students who view themselves as being more experienced or better qualified than the other students. Their belief in their own abilities, combined with the need to protect their self-image can lead them to being very defensive when their lack of knowledge is exposed. It must be remembered that they are likely to feel their whole self is under attack. The effect of this can be exacerbated when there is a great difference between the expertise of the educator and that of the student. Major conflict can rapidly ensue, and it is for the educator to understand and deal with what is happening. In some cases, it may be beyond the intellectual ability of the student to comprehend the factors at play and they will default to an ever increasingly defensive stance. If this is the case the better option may be for the educator to make a tactical retreat, then deal with the issue later and in an alternative way.

6.10 Bringing trauma to class

In an adult learning environment, the educator must be prepared to deal with the potential for something they are teaching to activate memories of previous trauma that a student has experienced. The very nature of trauma means that even the most innocuous comment or reference can trigger emotional pain. We can't keep this type of thing out of the classroom. It is not as if we can run the students through a 'trauma' scanner, as we would to prevent them bringing a knife or gun to the class. The linking of the learning to previous trauma is likely to create a block to learning for the student.

If the educator has a good knowledge of defense mechanisms, they are more likely to realize that the student is reacting to some previous trauma and not to the specific content of the lesson. The educator can then differentiate between what is a reaction to previous trauma (albeit stimulated by something in the lesson) and a reaction directly relating to the class. It is not necessary for the educator to know the specific nature of the trauma to overcome the problem, only to recognize that one may exist. A failure to identify that there is potentially underlying trauma, leaves the educator trying to deal with something they don't know is present.

While the classroom is not the place to discuss any such trauma, a quiet word after the class is appropriate, tactfully providing the student with options, without specifically stating the suspicion there may be an underlying issue. Often the worst thing for the student may be the thought that someone has seen what they have been trying to keep hidden.

6.11 Personal application

Much of this book has focused on understanding defense mechanisms in structured learning environments. However, this understanding has many more uses, and we begin with considering how it can help us in our personal life:

- Many of our reactions that our driven by defense mechanisms have a negative element; at best they are a temporary fix. If we understand how we react in certain circumstances, if we can put a label on what is driving the behavior and if we are aware of the negative impact that those reactions can have, then we are in a better position to take steps to modify our reactions. This can have a hugely positive effect on our personal relationships.

- Although we are not trying to be amateur psychologists, awareness of the concepts will allow us to us to identify the relevant behavior in others, thus giving us the option to make allowance for their behavior, rather than just reacting to it and creating greater conflict.

- Defense mechanisms can be viewed as being manipulative. The person, albeit unconsciously attempts to change another's view of the reality. If we are aware of the way defense mechanisms work, we are less likely to fall victim to these machinations. We can think of ways to allow the person to protect their ego, while at the same time, protecting ourselves from manipulation.

6.12 Workplace Application

Moving on from but including the personal life applications, there are many times that this new knowledge can help us in the work place:

- New experiences. Often in the work place we encounter new experiences. These have the potential to threaten the sense of who we are – our sense of self. This threat can be reduced by accepting that we will always encounter new experiences and our sense of self can change without being critically damaged. By viewing the self as continuously undergoing a process of evolution it becomes easier to accept new experiences.

- Change. We don't like change. Implicit in change is risk; risk to our safety. We like when things stay the same to the extent that even if things are barely tolerable, we would rather they stayed the same than change. People would rather stay in hell because at least there, they know the names of the streets. When encountering change we will feel under threat and are more likely to utilize defense mechanisms. If we are responsible for implementing change, we are very likely to encounter defense mechanisms used against us. The greater the change, the greater threat and the more likely our staff are to resort to defense mechanisms. As managers, understanding what is going on, allows us to put in place strategies to counter the negative effects. As with new experiences if we don't accept change, the alternative is to defend against it by denying or distorting (consciously or unconsciously) what is threatening to us.

- Continuous development. In most work places it is beneficial to have a culture that promotes staff development and openness. While training courses form part of this, it is much healthier if every day is looked upon as a learning day, and staff become habituated to that type of environment, as opposed to continually defending against it. However, it must be borne in mind that some people will feel continuously unnerved in such a climate.

- Generational change. With each generation comes change and this can result in inter-generational conflict in the work place. How often have we heard 'baby boomers' regale against the attitude of 'millennials' often distorting the reality of how it was in their day. One of the things that remains constant is that we all have egos and we all use mechanisms to defend those egos. The circumstances and the actual way we employ them may vary but the actual mechanisms are the same.

6.13 Hard lines

This book should end with a conclusion; a nice way to bring everything together and leave us all feeling so much wiser and better about life. Instead, it seems more appropriate to end with a few simple thoughts:

- When a castle is under a siege, the longer it goes on the harder things get, and before long we are eating each other. So, it is with defense mechanisms, if we are under siege, we use them too much and they eat us from the inside.
- We are not special; we are not entitled to anything. No matter how many Facebook friends we have or followers on Instagram, we are just

the same as everyone else. If you are an only child, you may be special to your parents; if you are not, you are not even special to them. Get over it. Nothing makes us more vulnerable to life's ups and downs than an expectation that we are somehow different and should be treated accordingly.

- Sometimes we do stupid things. Sometimes we do bad things. But this doesn't make us stupid or bad.

- Pain has its purpose. It pushes us to find solutions.

- If we are struggling, tell someone, everything. If it's a friend they will want to help, if it's a stranger what have you to lose. Talking out our feelings helps us gain perspective.

- Bad things happen to people, but we can always be sure something worse has happened to someone else. Try not to take life too seriously. It's not personal; it happens to all of us.

- Be a bit more understanding – tomorrow it might be your life that sucks.

AUTHOR'S 2ND NOTE

I f you haven't enjoyed this book…And I know this won't have happened, but if you haven't, I know it is not my fault. I am a highly regarded international author. It is probably because you are not smart enough. If you find mistakes it is because the editor has missed them, not me. And if there is one thing, I can't stand it is people who don't pay attention to detail. Furthermore, if there hadn't been so many people wanting to read it, I would have taken more time to include more in it. Who says 'size matters'?

And anyway, I don't care what you think. I am going to medicate with beer. And no, I don't have a drinking problem. I am just not feeling well. I might go back to bed where I will curl up under the quilt and hide. If anyone comes near me my teddy bear will attack them. And he is very big and very fierce.

REFERENCES

Beck, A. T. (1976). Cognitive therapies and emotional disorders. New York: New American Library.

Burns, D. D. (2012). Feeling good: The new mood therapy. New York: New American Library.

Cambridge Dictionary (2108) Available at: https://dictionary.cambridge.org/dictionary/english/defence-mechanism Accessed May 2018

Collins Dictionary (2018) Available at: https://www.collinsdictionary.com/dictionary/english/defence-mechanism Accessed May 2018

Cramer, P (2009) Seven Pillars of Defence Mechanism Theory [Paper presented on June 13, 2009, at the Annual Meeting of the Rapaport-Klein Study Group] Available at: http://www.psychomedia.it/rapaport-klein/cramer09.pdf

Accessed May 2018

Davanloo, H. (2000). Intensive Short-Term Dynamic Psychotherapy: Selected Papers of Habib Davanloo, MD. Chichester: John Wiley & Sons.

English Oxford Living Dictionary (2018a) Available at: https://en.oxforddictionaries.com/definition/guilt

Accessed April 2018

English Oxford Living Dictionary (2018b) Available at: https://en.oxforddictionaries.com/definition/shame

Accessed April 2018

Festinger, L. (1957). A Theory of Cognitive Dissonance. Stanford, CA: Stanford University Press.

Fossum, M. A.; Mason, Marilyn J. (1986), Facing Shame: Families in Recovery, W.W. Norton, p. 5, ISBN 0-393-30581-3

Gotink, R.A., Chu, P., Busschbach, J.J.V., Benson H. Fricchione, G.L., Hunink, M.M.G (2016) Standardised Mindfulness-Based Interventions in Healthcare: An Overview of Systematic Reviews and Meta-Analyses of RCTs. Available at: http://jour-nals.plos.org/plosone/article?id=10.1371/jour-nal.pone.0124344 Accessed Jan 2019

Kantor, M. (2002), Passive-aggression: a guide for the therapist, the patient and the victim, Westport, CT: Praeger Publishers

Kruger, Justin; Dunning, David (1999). "Unskilled and Unaware of It: How Difficulties in Recognizing One's Own Incompetence Lead to Inflated Self-Assessments". Journal of Personality and Social Psychology. American Psychological Association. 77 (6): 1121–1134.

Freud, S. (1961) The ego and the id. In. Strachey (Ed. and Trans.), The standard edition of the complete works of Sigmund Freud (Vol. 19, pp. 12-66). London: Hogarth Press.

Malone, J. C., Cohen, S., Liu, S. R., Vaillant, G. E., & Waldinger, R. J. (2013). Adaptive midlife defence mechanisms and late-life health. Personality and Individual Differences, 55(2), 85–89.

McNally, R. J. (2007). Mechanisms of exposure therapy: how neuroscience can improve psychological treatments for anxiety disorders. Clinical Psychology Review 27, 750–759

Merriam S. B (1984) Developmental issues and tasks of young adulthood. New Directions for Adult and Continuing Education Volume 1984 issue 21 3-13

Mezirow, J. (2009). Transformative learning theory. In J. Mezirow, and E. W. Taylor (Eds), Transformative Learning in Practise: Insights from Community. San Francisco, CA: Jossey-Bass.

Moze, M.B. (2007). Surrender: An Alchemical Act in Personal Transformation. Journal of Conscious Evolution, 1-46.

Reber, A.S., & Reber, E. (2002). The Penguin dictionary of psychology. New York: Penguin Books.

Rubin, K.H. Coplan, R.J. and Bowker J.C. (2009) Social Withdrawal in Childhood. Annual Review of Psychology. 2009; 60: 141–171. Available at https://www.ncbi.nlm.nih.gov/pmc/articles/PMC3800115/

Accessed May 2018

Steele, C. M. (1988). The psychology of self-affirmation: Sustaining the integrity of the self. Advances in Experimental Social Psychology, 21, 261-302

Tangney, J. P. (1995). Shame and guilt in interpersonal relationships. In J. P. Tangney & K. W. Fischer (Eds.), Self-conscious emotions: Shame, guilt, embarrassment, and pride (pp. 114– 139). New York: Guilford Press

Vaillant, G E. (1992) Ego Mechanisms of Defence: A Guide for Clinicians and Researchers. American Psychiatric Publishing.

BY THE SAME AUTHOR

The human source management system – The use of psychology in the management of human intelligence sources. (2006)

Invest now or pay later – The management of risk in covert law enforcement. (2008)

Managing intelligence – A guide for law enforcement professionals. (2015)

For more information visit our website at:
WWW.HSMTRAINING.COM

Printed in Great Britain
by Amazon